2	**Detroit Rock City**
13	**King Of The Night Time World**
21	**God Of Thunder**
25	**Great Expectations**
31	**Flaming Youth**
38	**Sweet Pain**
46	**Shout It Out Loud**
53	**Beth**
57	**Do You Love Me**

ISBN 978-1-4234-0416-3

7777 W. BLUEMOUND RD. P.O. BOX 13819 MILWAUKEE, WI 53213

For all works contained herein:
Unauthorized copying, arranging, adapting,
recording or public performance is an infringement of copyright.
Infringers are liable under the law.

Visit Hal Leonard Online at
www.halleonard.com

Detroit Rock City

Words and Music by Paul Stanley and Bob Ezrin

Tune down 1/2 step:
(low to high) Eb-Ab-Db-Gb-Bb-Eb

Intro
Fast Rock ♩ = 184

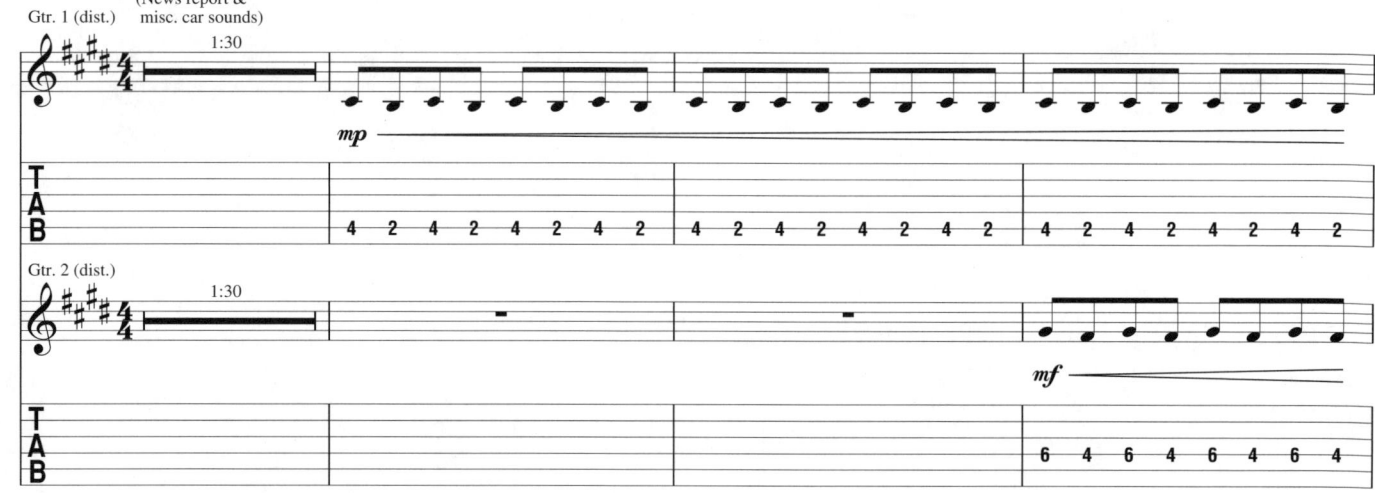

*Chord symbols reflect implied harmony.

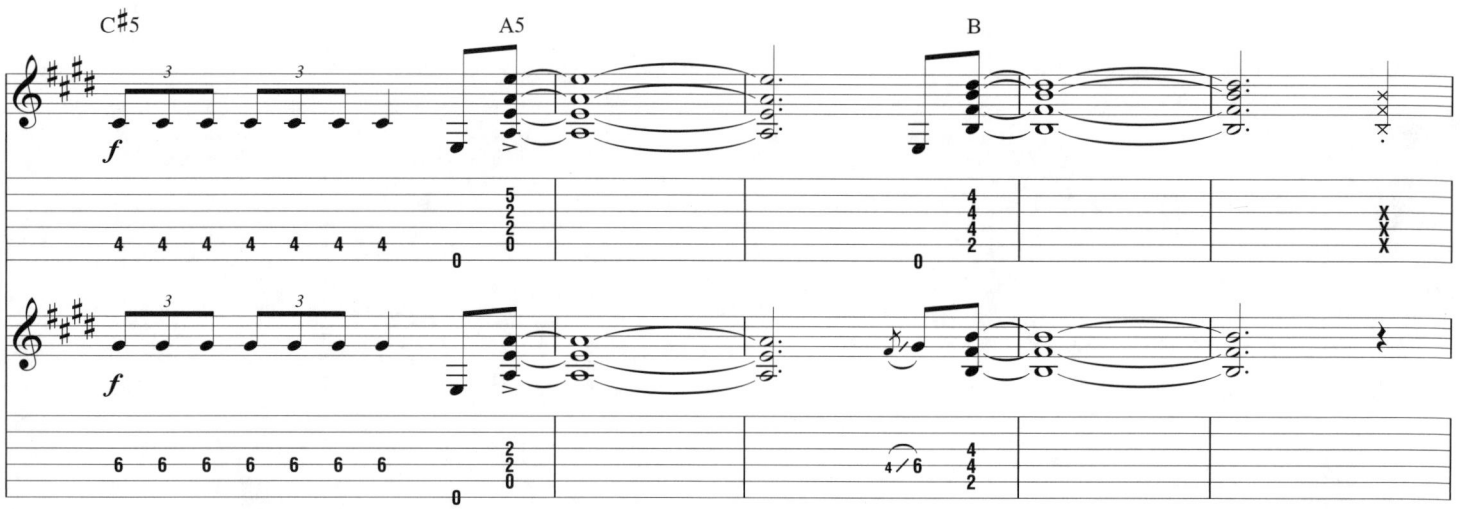

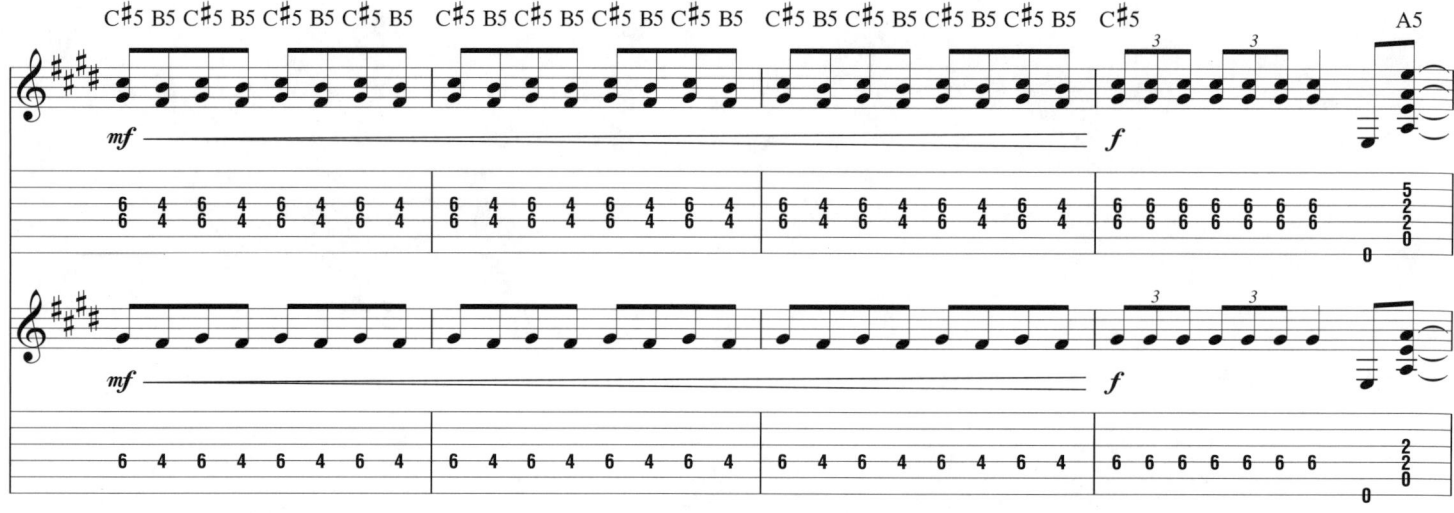

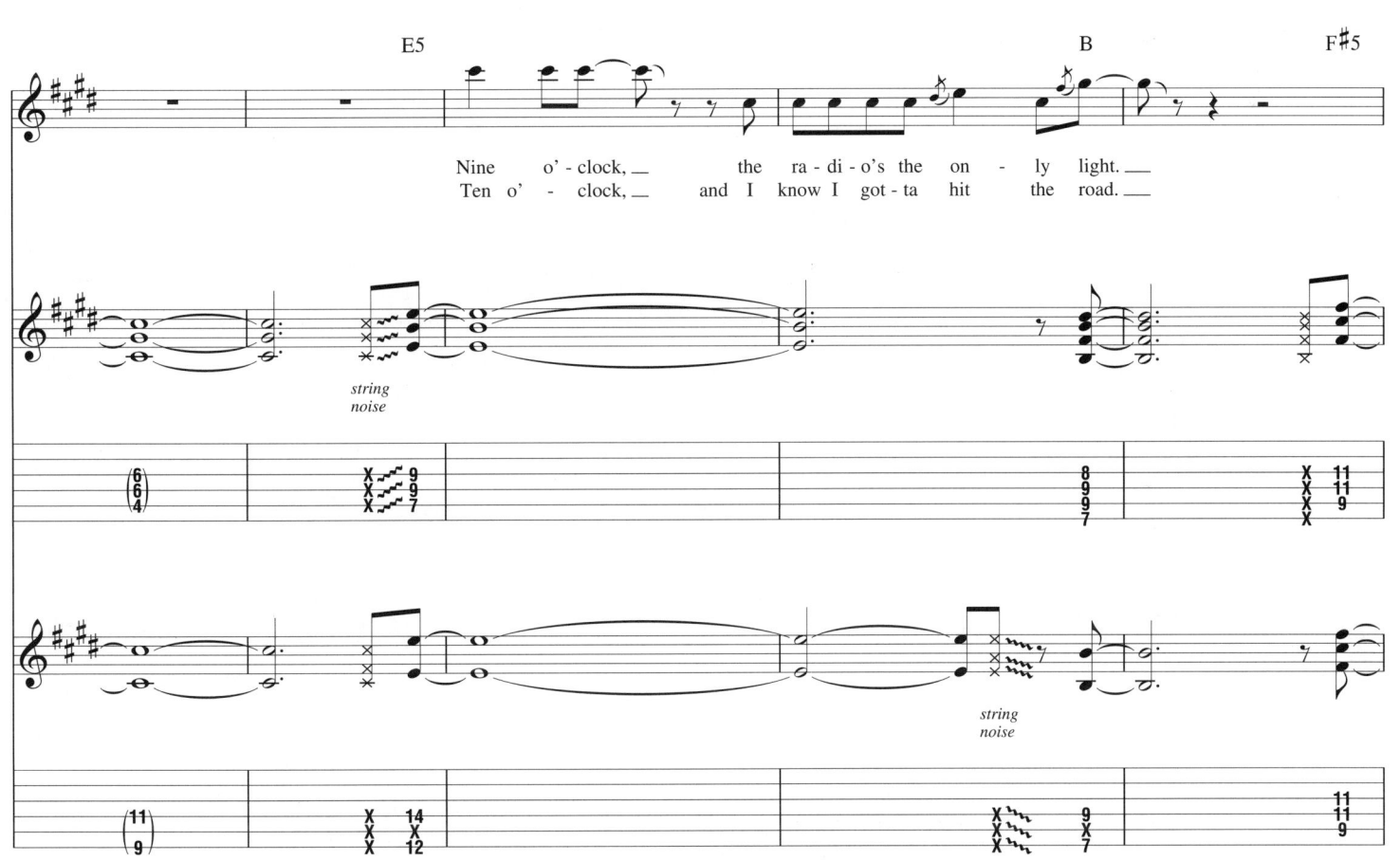

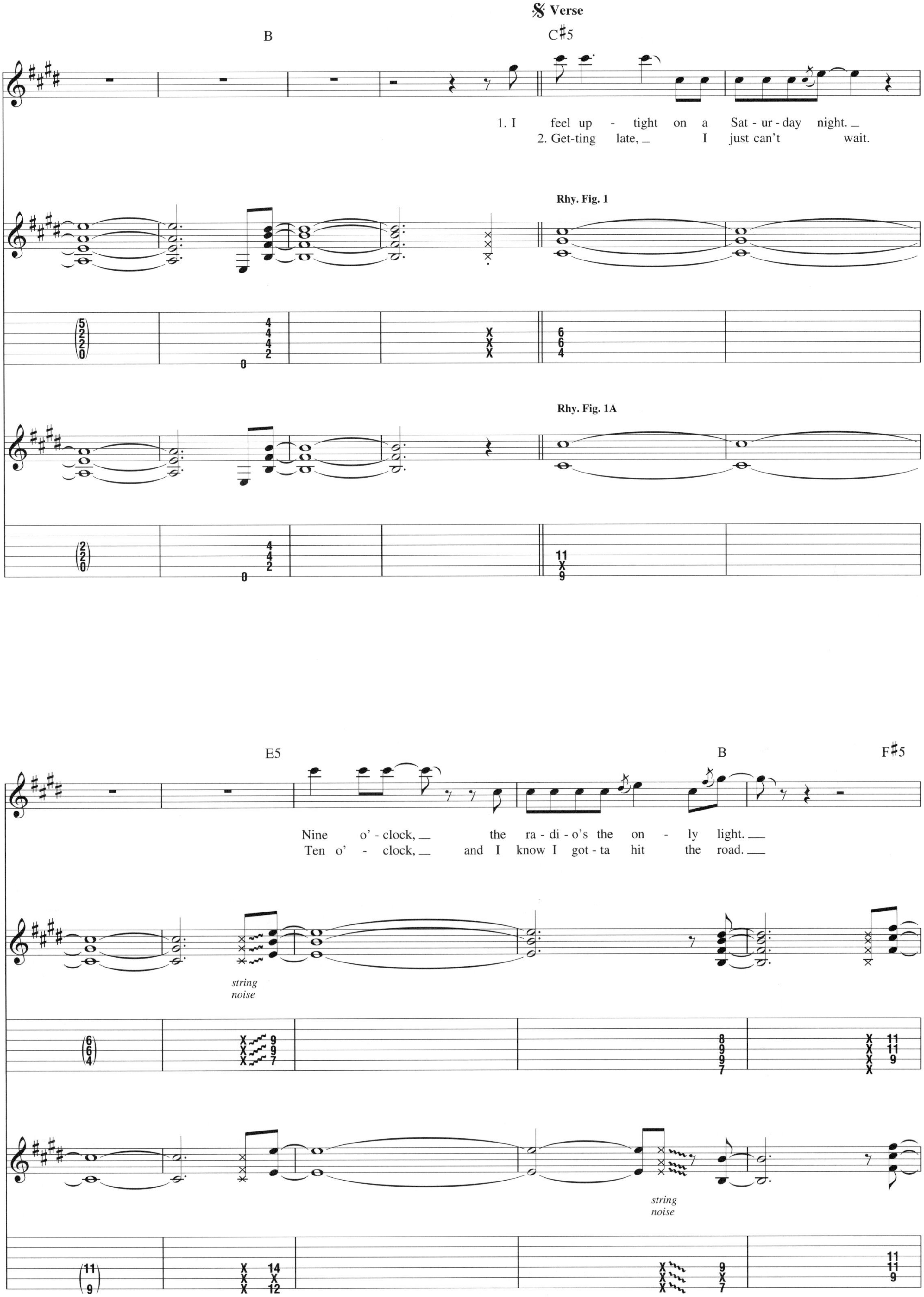

C♯5
E5
I hear my song __ and it pulls me through. __
First I drink, then I smoke,
B
F♯5
A5
Comes on strong, tells me what I got - ta do. ________ I got ___ to...
start up the car __ and I try to make the mid-night show. ______ (Get up!) _
End Rhy. Fig. 1
End Rhy. Fig. 1A

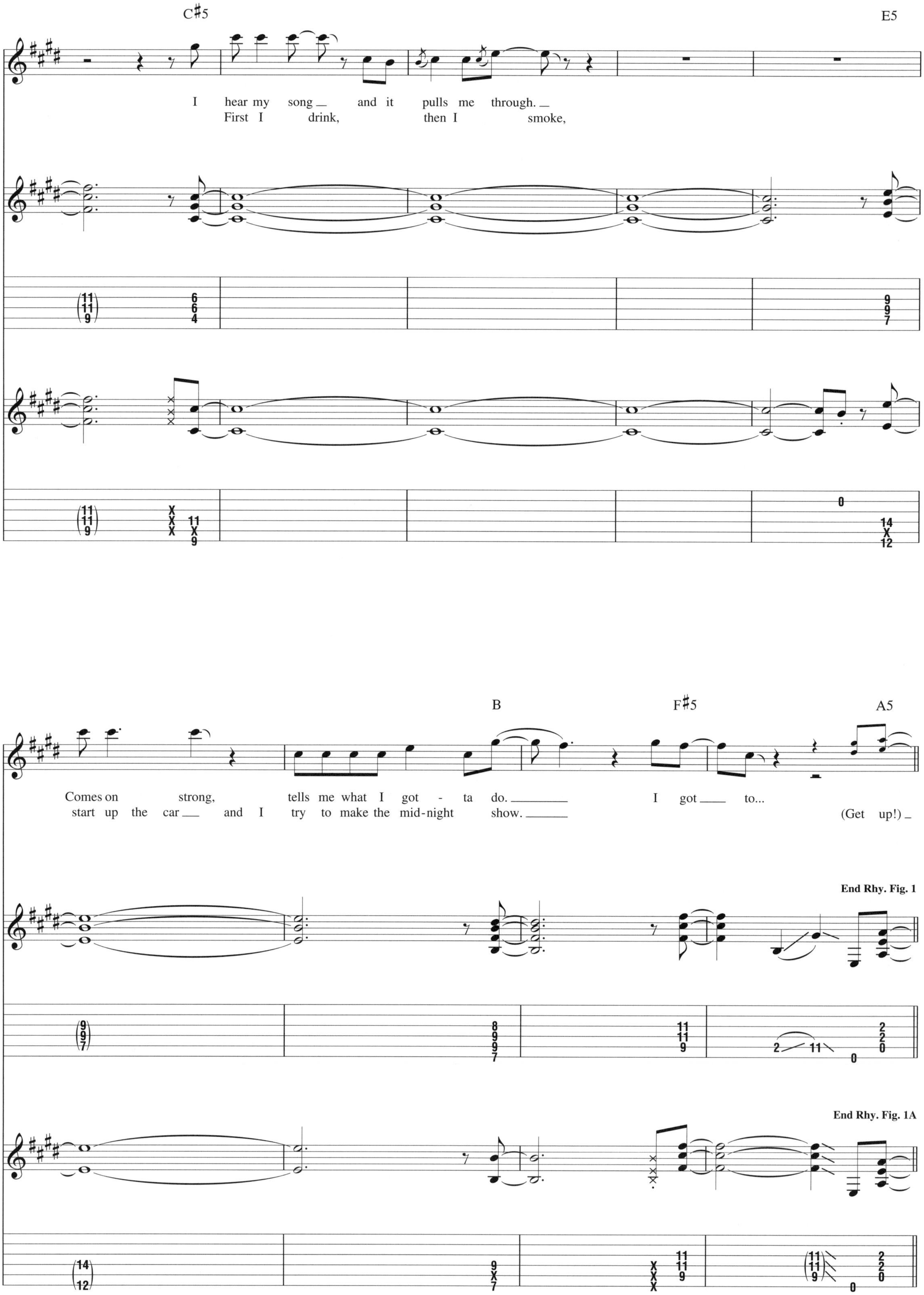

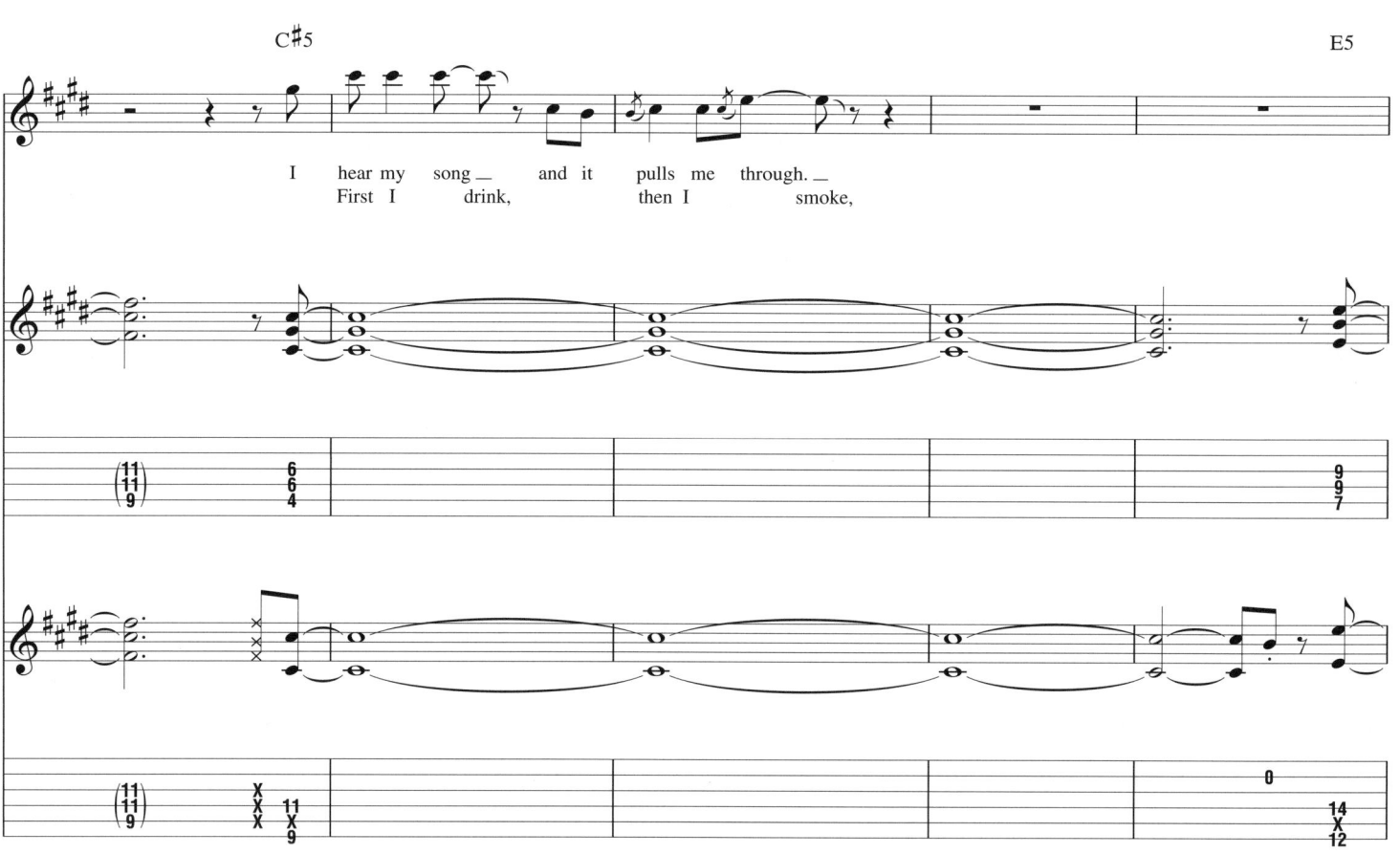

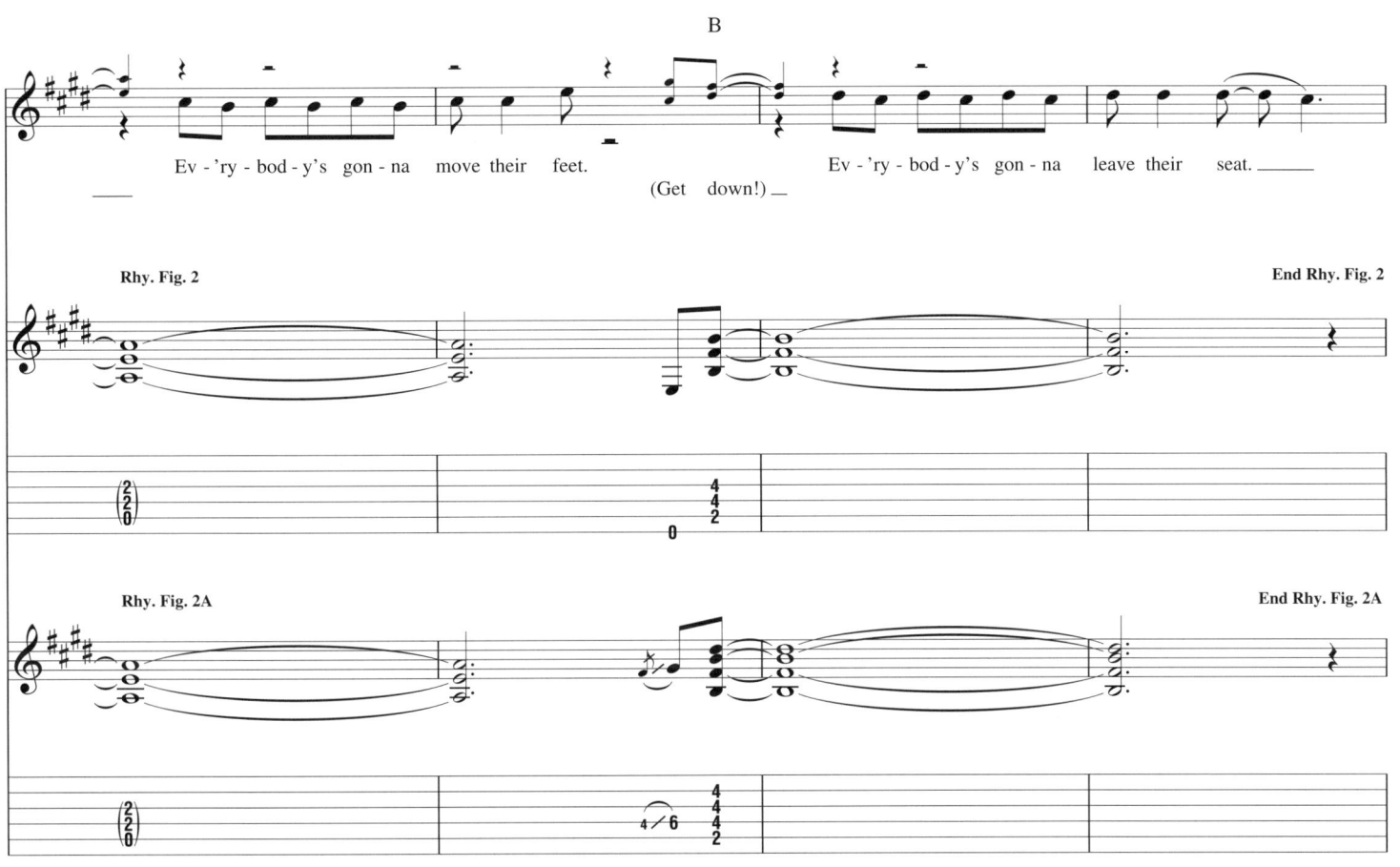

C#5
A5
Gtr. 6
Gtr. 5
Gtr. 4
Gtr. 3
Gtrs. 1 & 2
Gtrs. 1 & 2: w/ Rhy. Figs. 2 & 2A
B
Gtrs. 1 & 2: w/ Riff A
N.C.

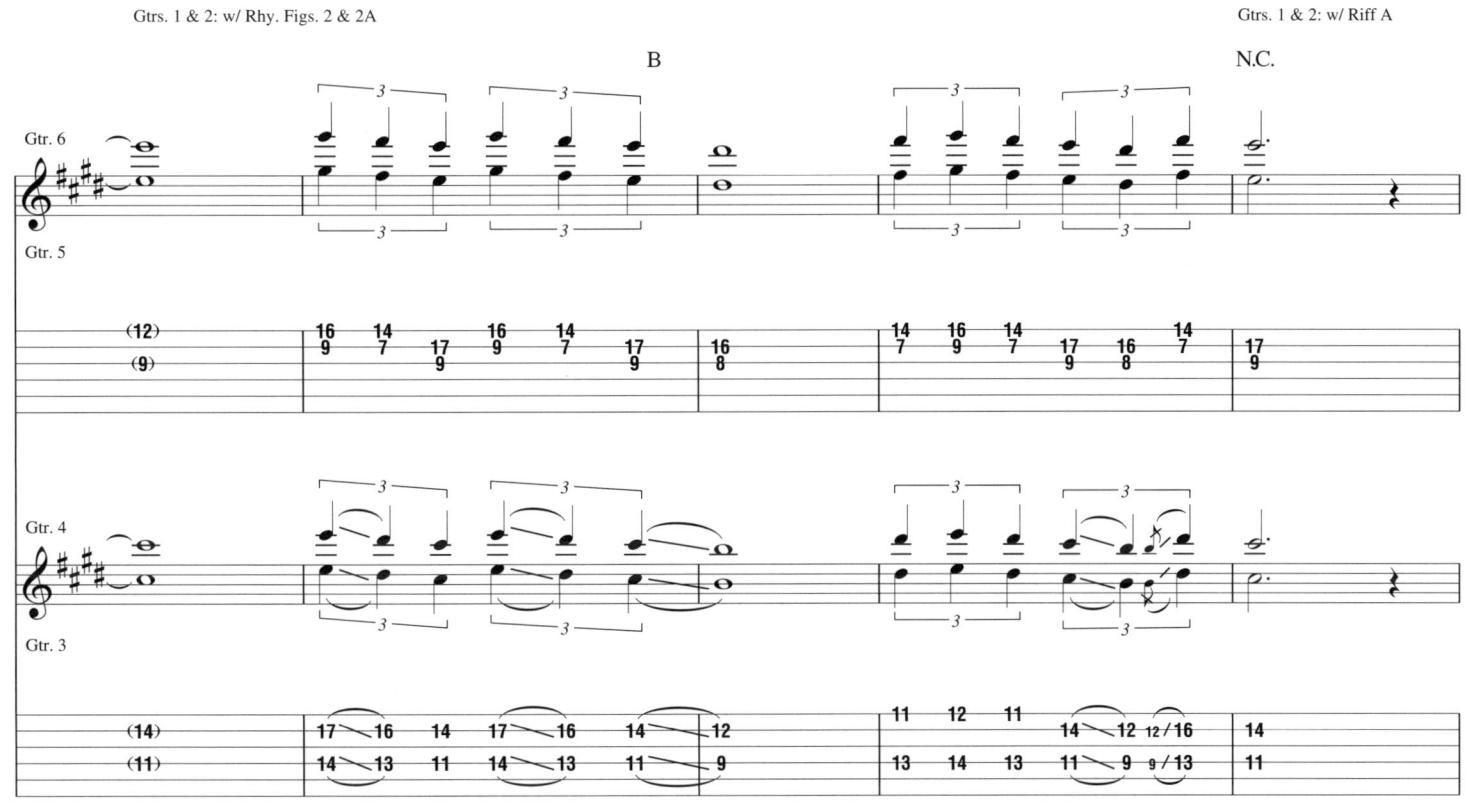

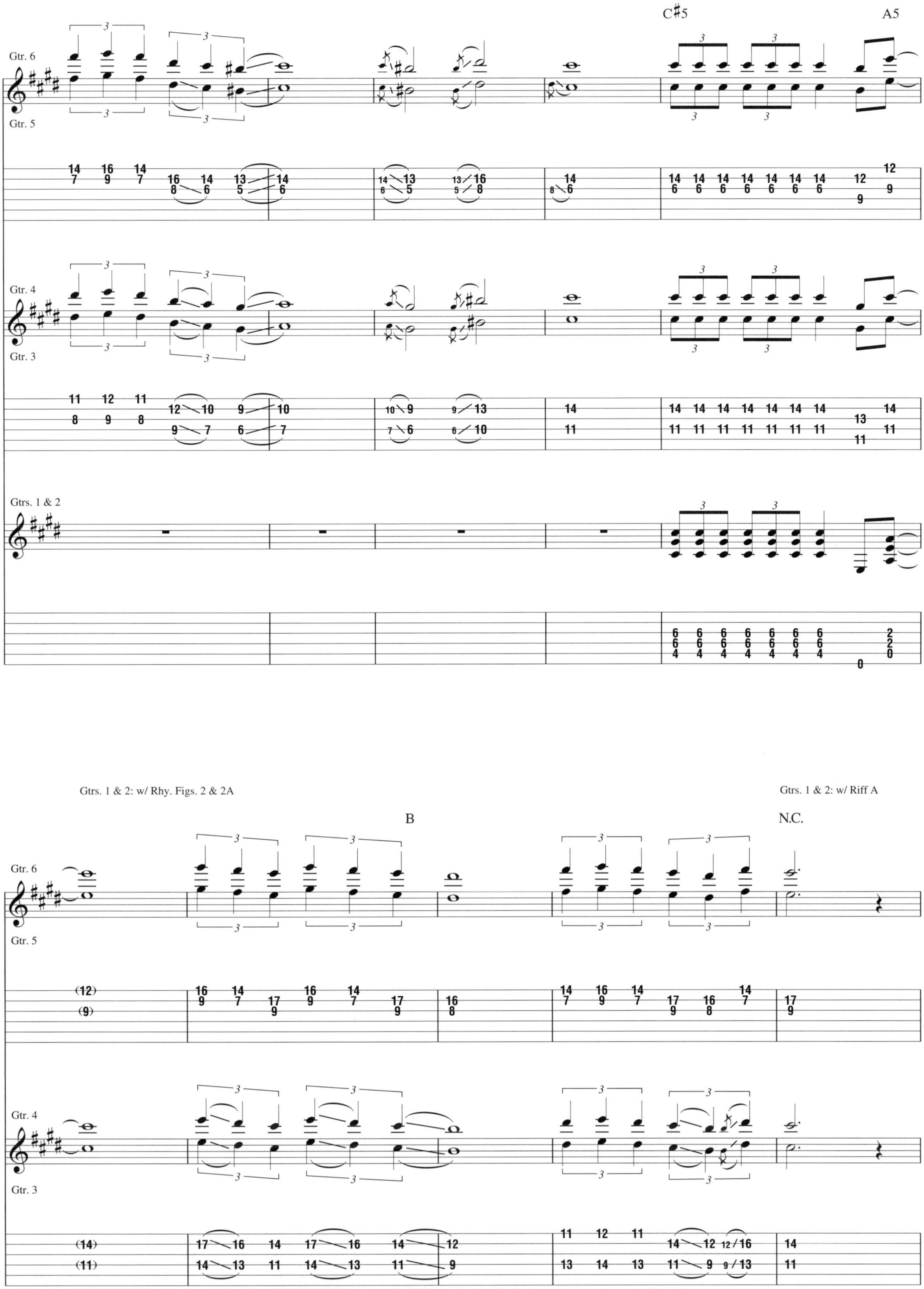

Gtrs. 1 & 2: w/ Rhy. Figs. 2 & 2A
A5
B
Gtr. 6
8va
loco
Gtr. 5
Gtr. 4
Gtr. 3
Verse
Gtr. 1: w/ Rhy. Fig. 1
Gtr. 2: w/ Riff B
Gtrs. 5 & 6 tacet
C♯5
4. Twelve o' - clock, I got - ta rock.
Gtr. 6
Gtr. 5
divisi
Gtr. 4
Gtr. 3

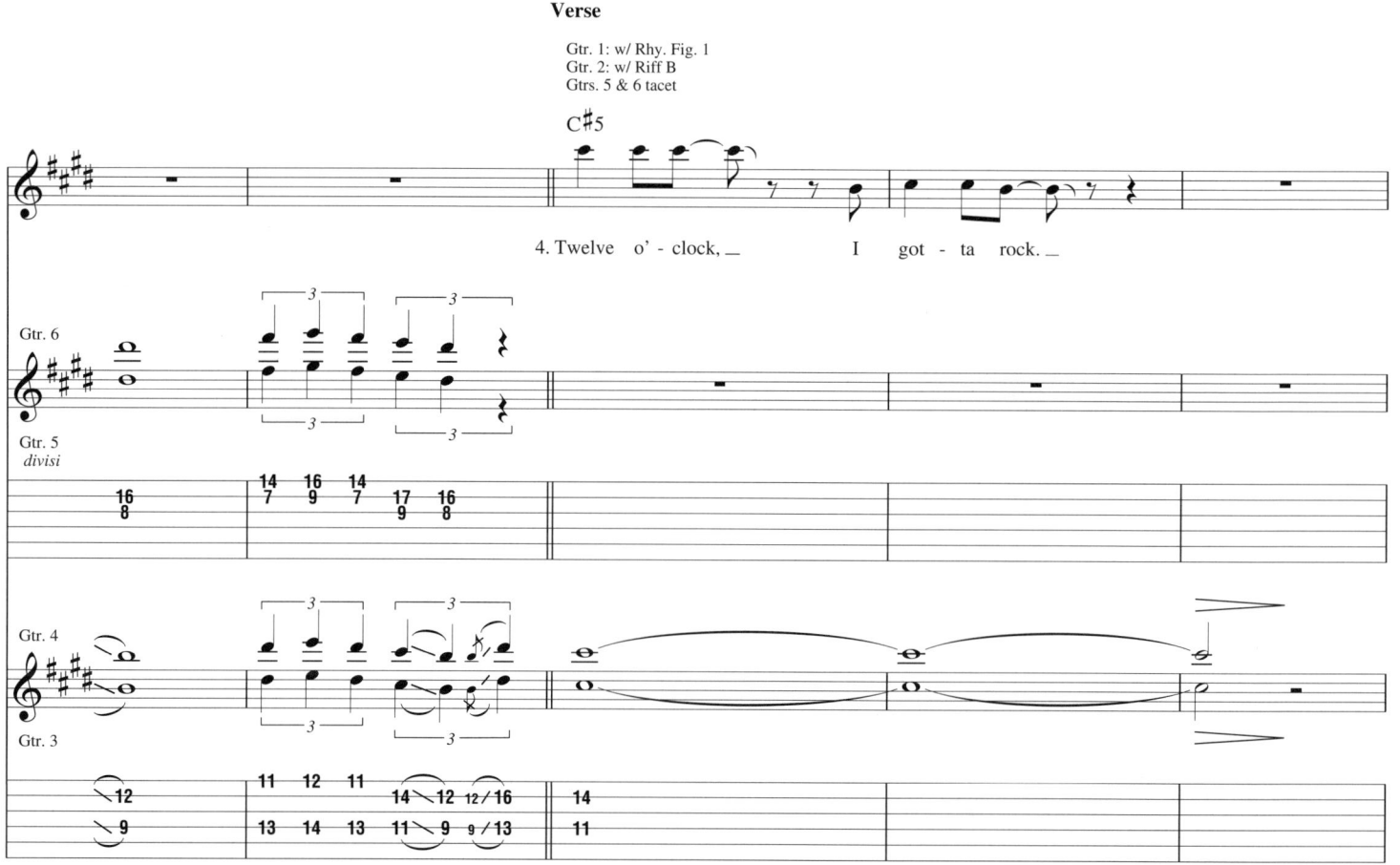

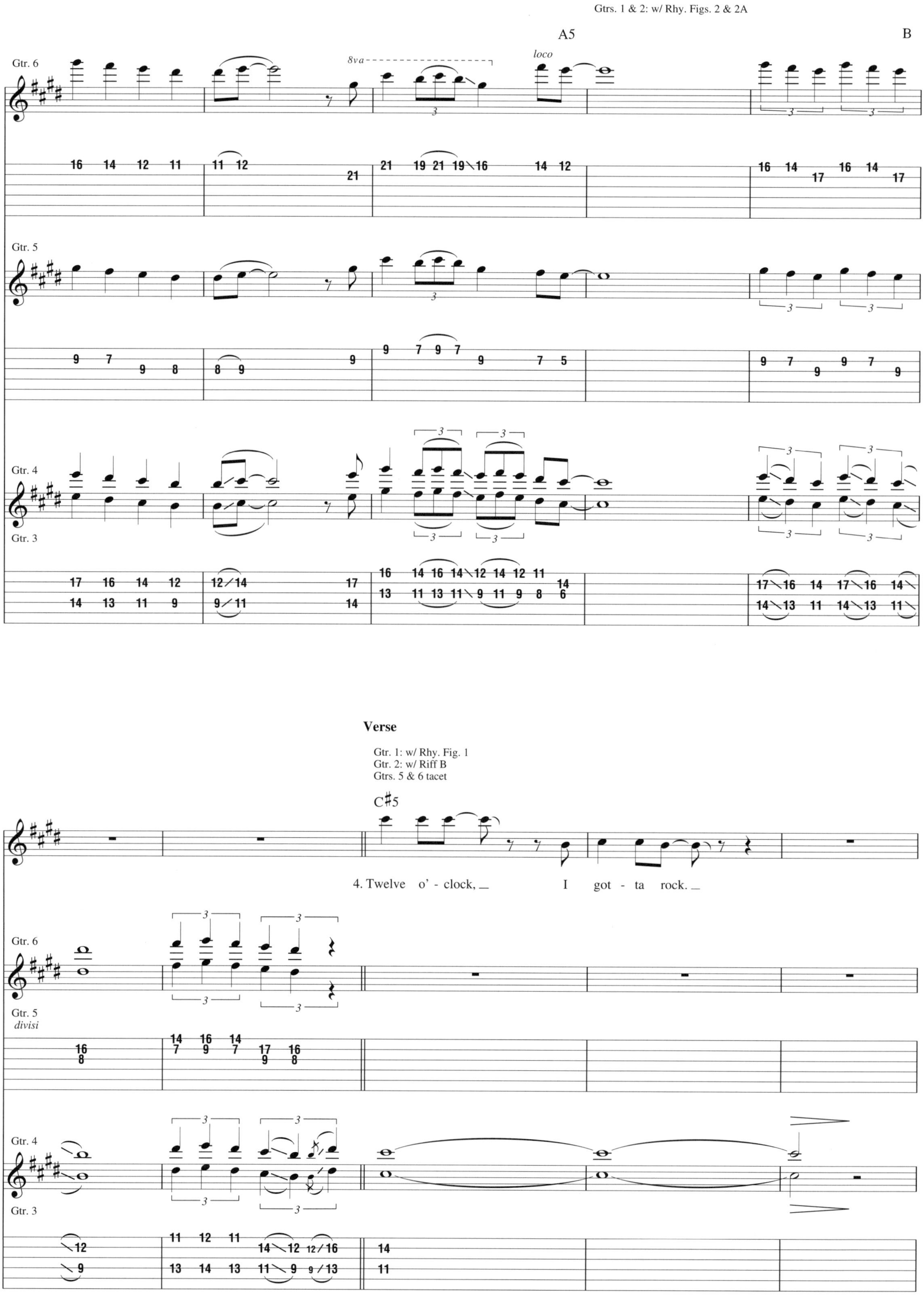

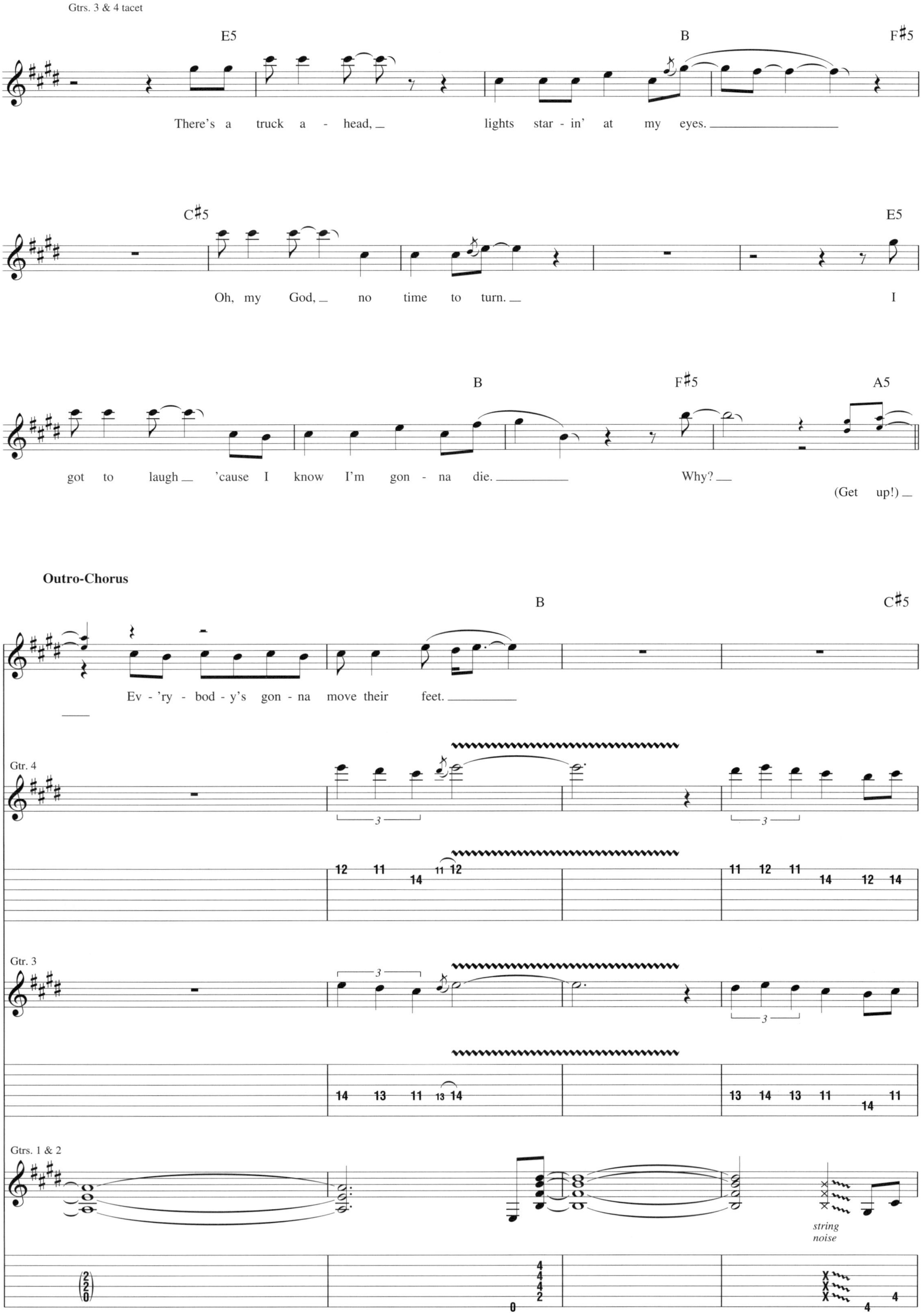

There's a truck a-head, lights star-in' at my eyes.

Oh, my God, no time to turn. I

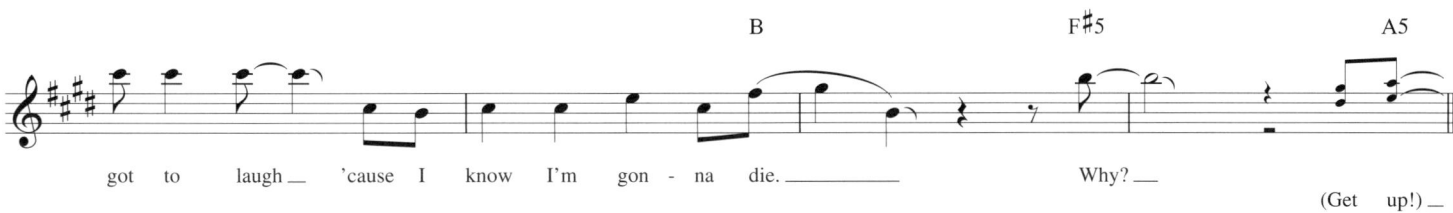

got to laugh 'cause I know I'm gon-na die. Why?
(Get up!)

Outro-Chorus

Ev-'ry-bod-y's gon-na move their feet.

Gtrs. 3 & 4 tacet
N.C.
E5 A5
Ev - 'ry - bod - y's gon - na
(Get up!)
Gtrs. 1 & 2
B
C♯5
(Car crash)
leave their seat.
Gtr. 6
Gtr. 5
divisi
Gtr. 3
Gtr. 4
divisi
Gtrs. 1 & 2

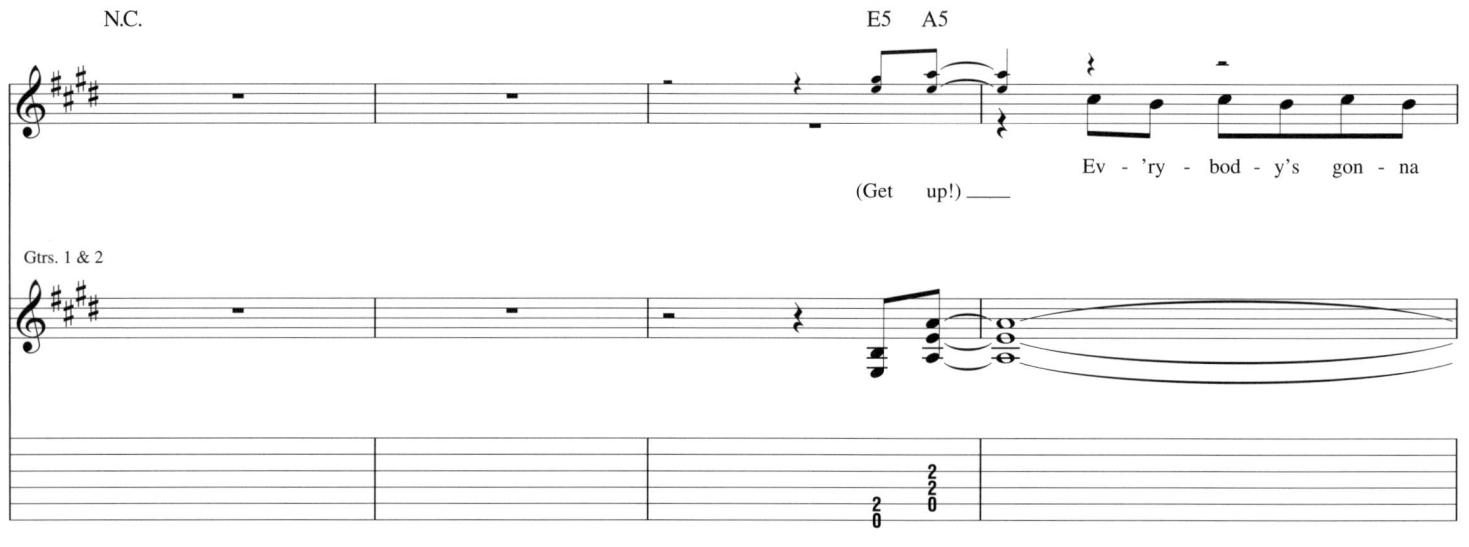

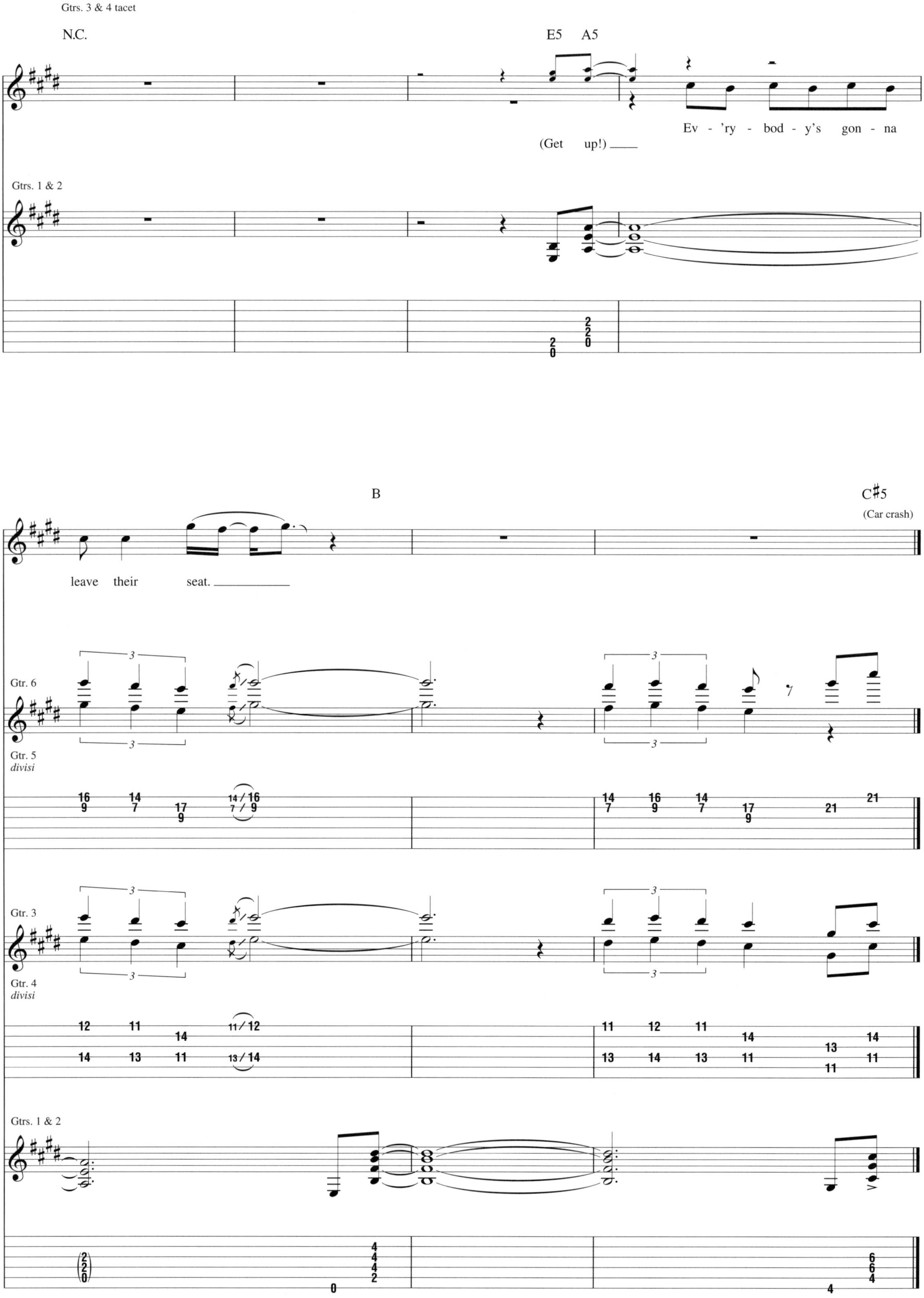

King of the Night Time World

Words and Music by Paul Stanley, Bob Ezrin, Kim Fowley and Mark Anthony

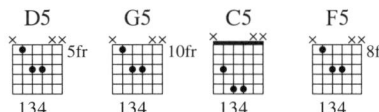

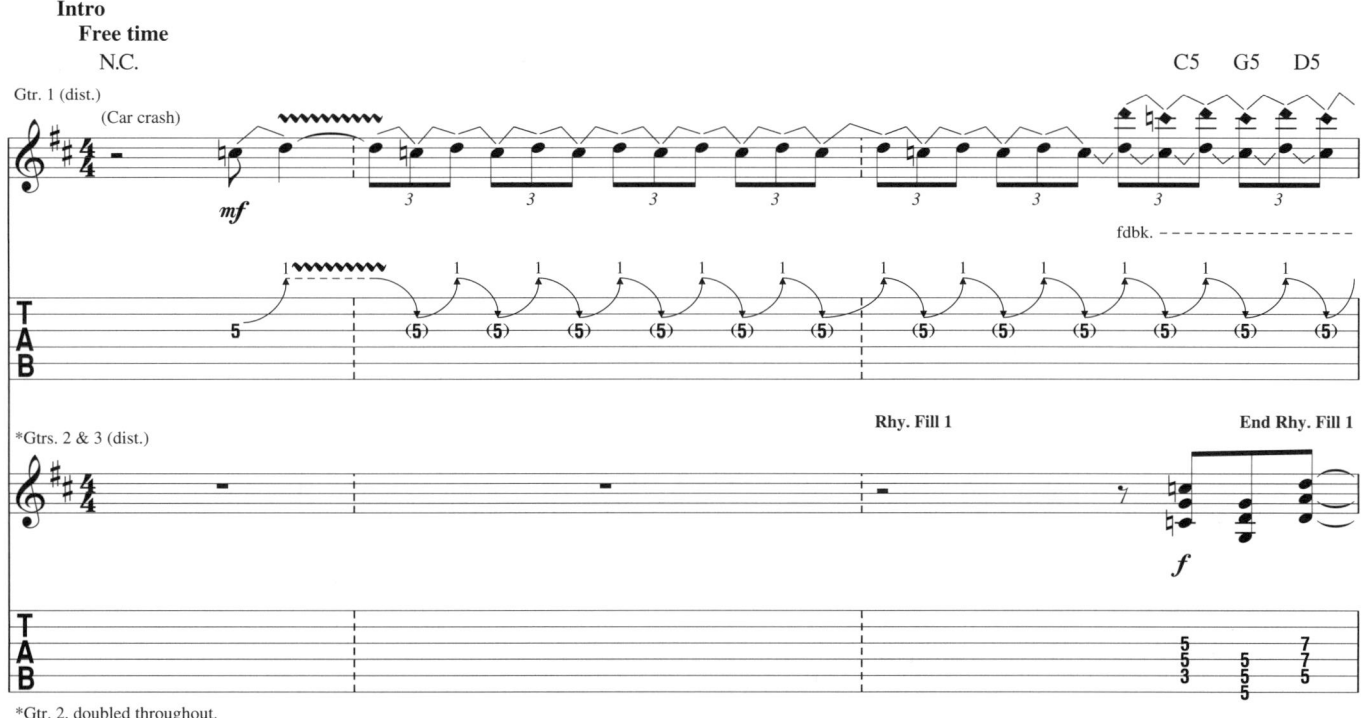

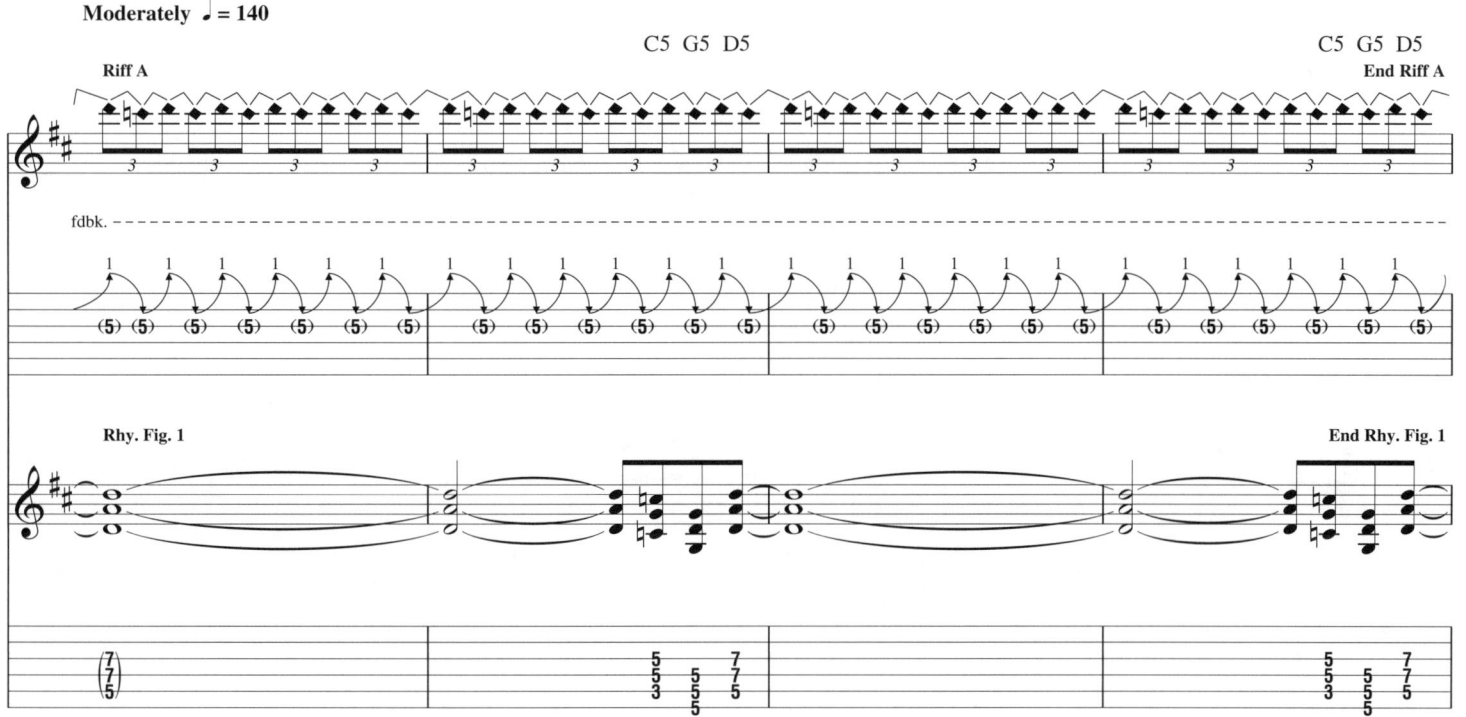

Copyright © 1976 HORI PRODUCTIONS AMERICA, INC., ALL BY MYSELF MUSIC, CAFE AMERICANA,
PEERMUSIC LTD., SCREEN GEMS-EMI MUSIC INC. and 8TH POWER MUSIC
Copyright Renewed
All Rights for HORI PRODUCTIONS AMERICA, INC. and ALL BY MYSELF MUSIC Controlled and Administered by
UNIVERSAL - POLYGRAM INTERNATIONAL PUBLISHING, INC.
All Rights for CAFE AMERICANA in the U.S. Administered by INTERSONG U.S.A., INC.
All Rights for 8TH POWER MUSIC Controlled and Administered by SCREEN GEMS-EMI MUSIC INC.
All Rights Reserved   Used by Permission

*Chord symbols reflect overall harmony.

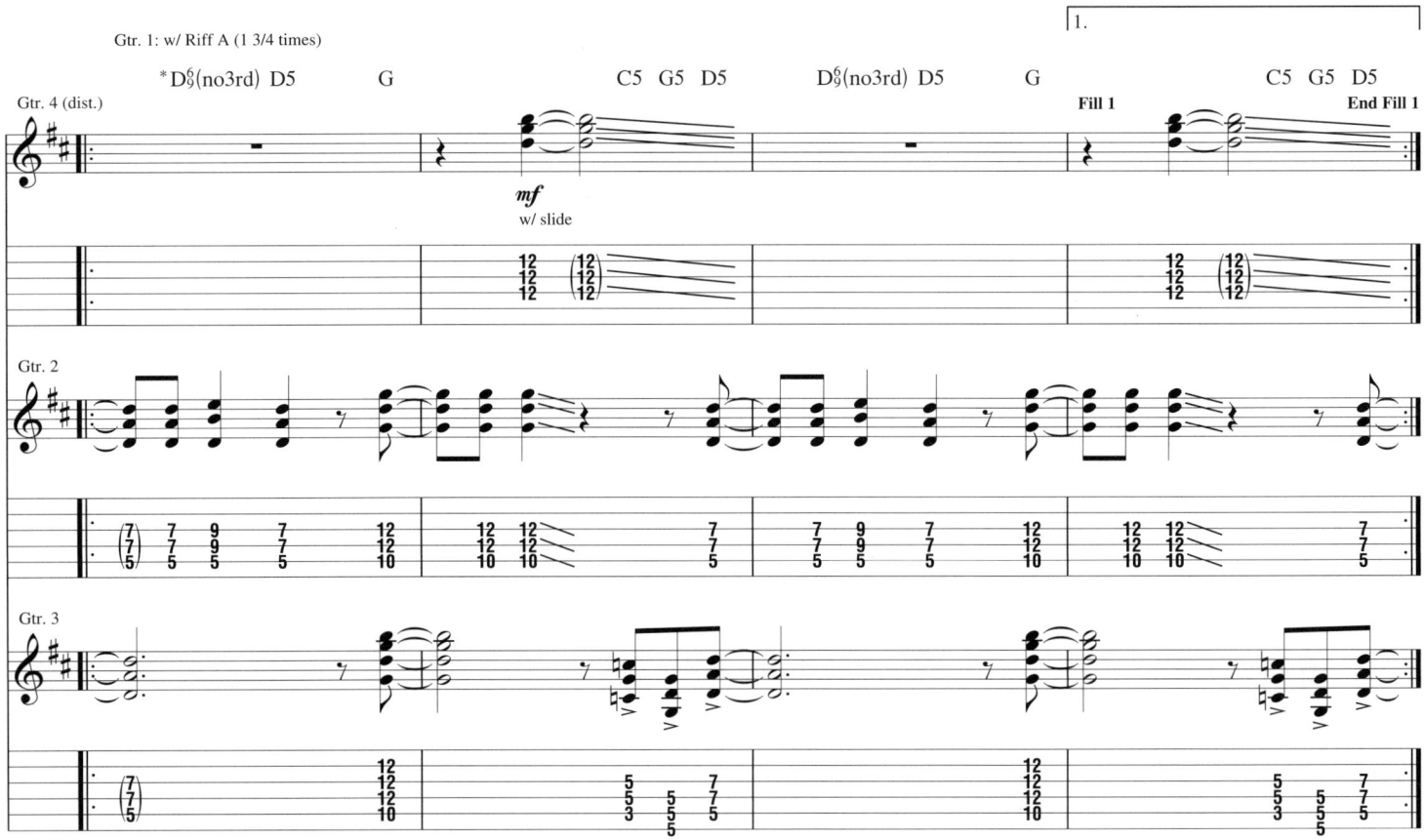

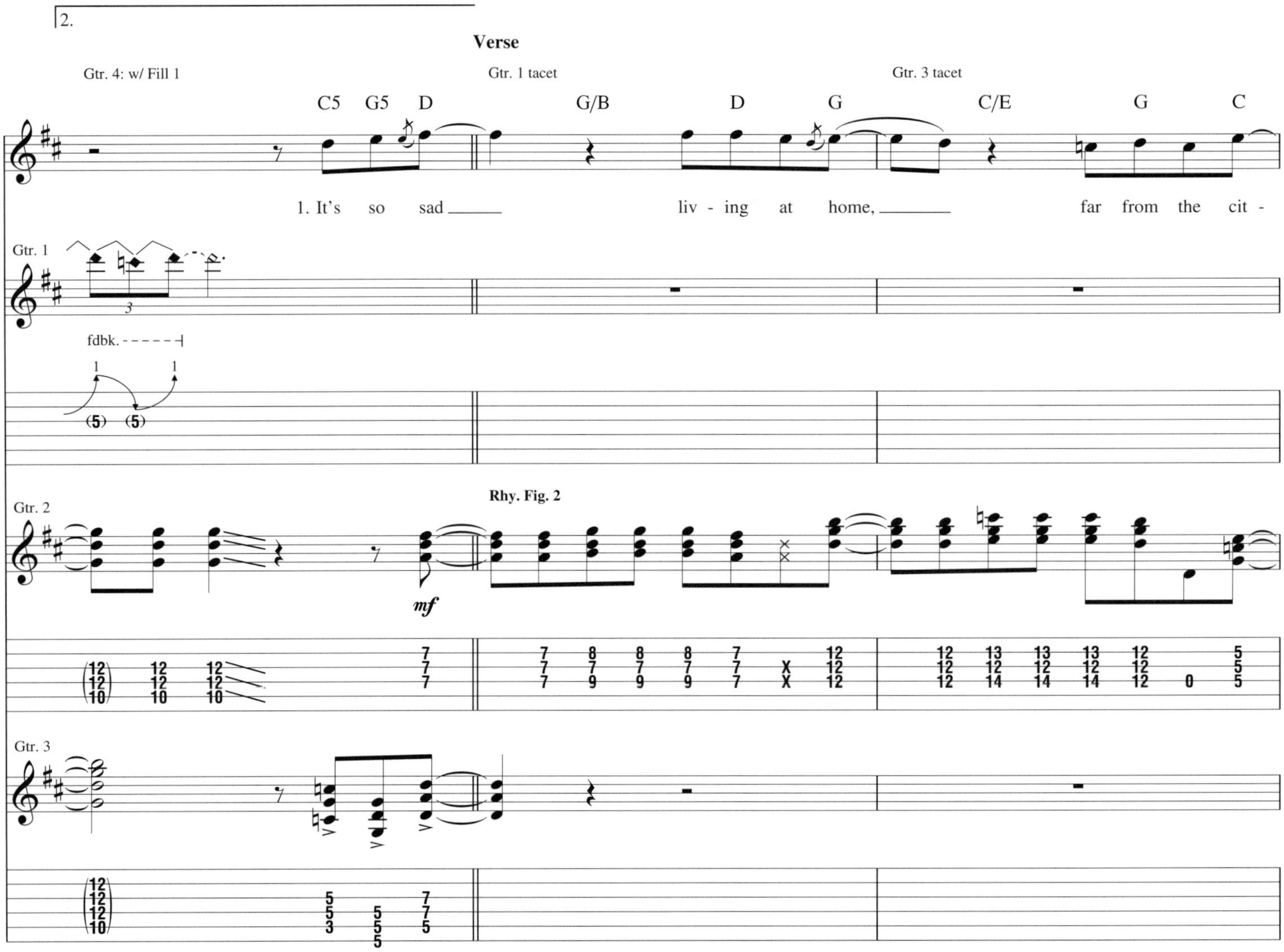

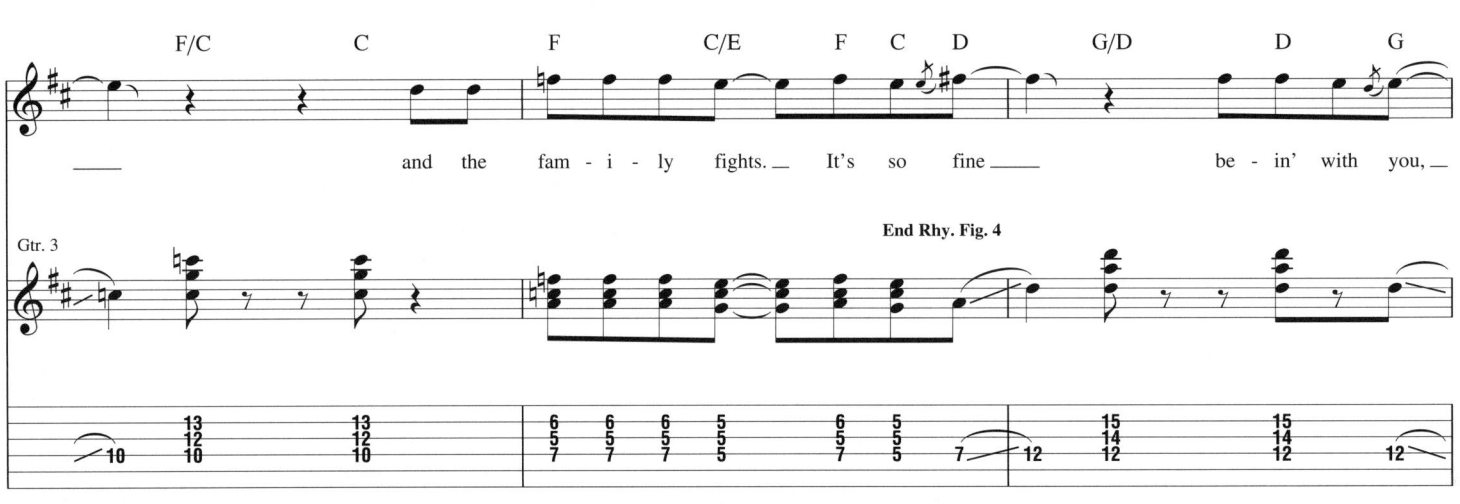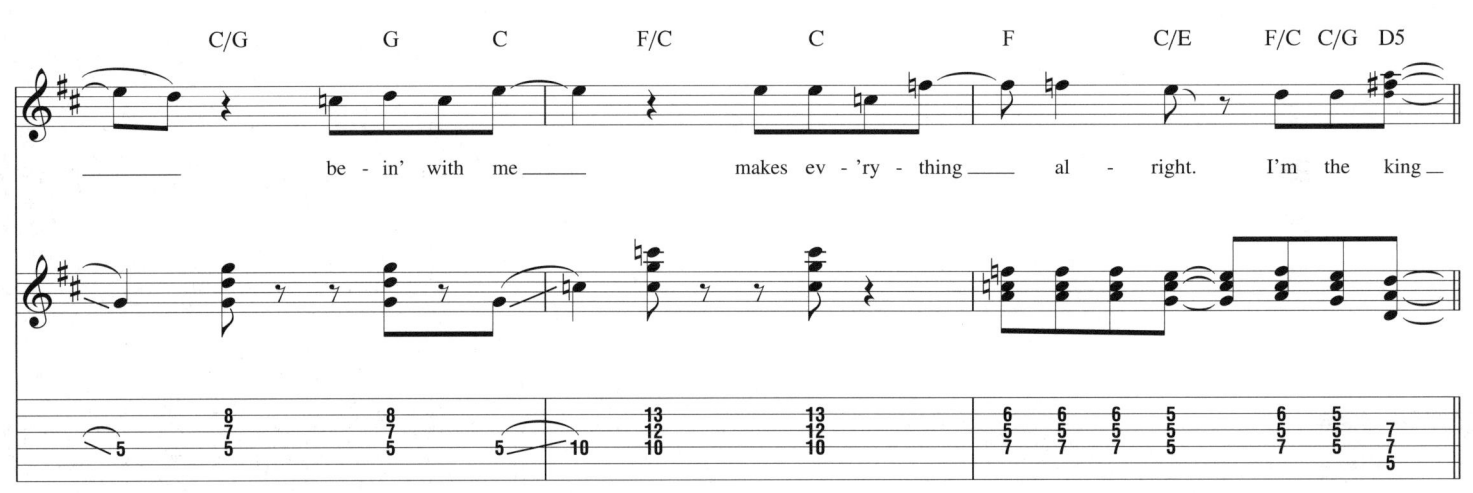

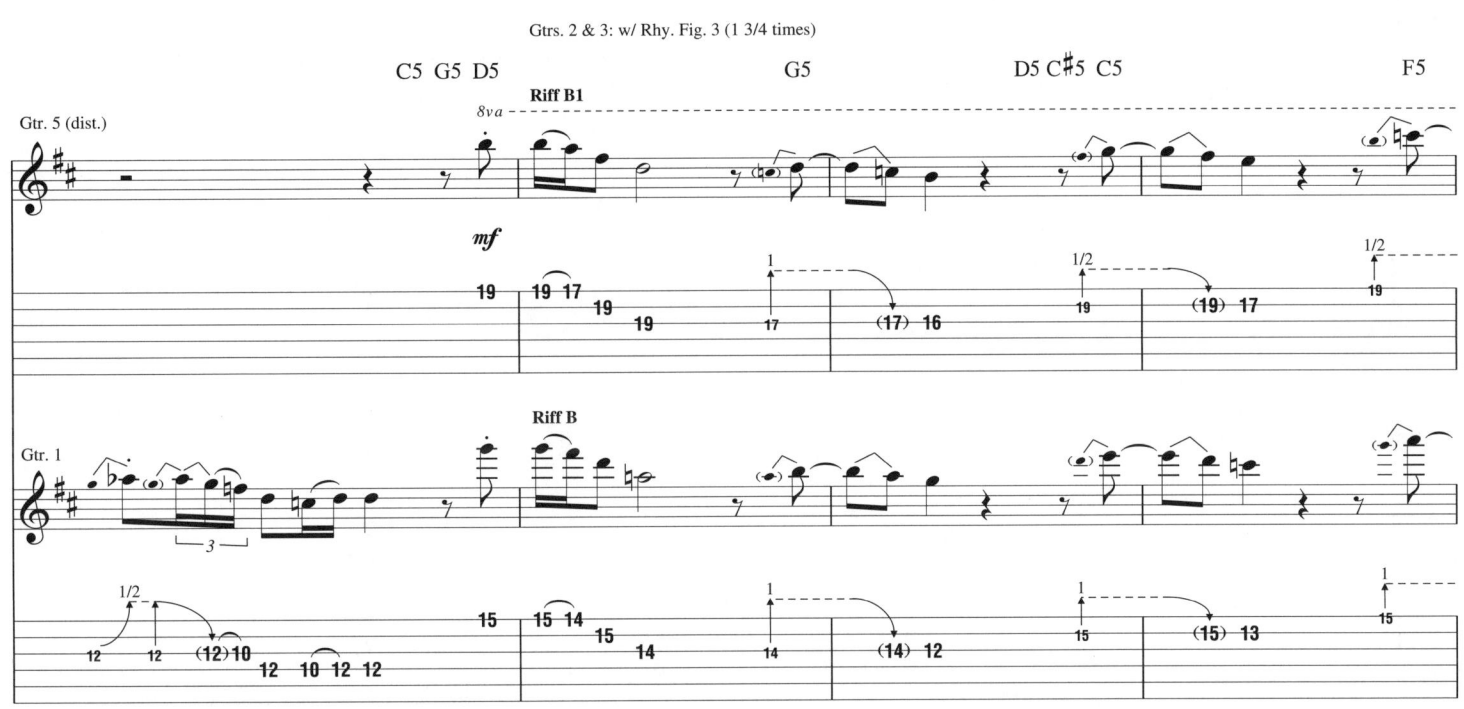

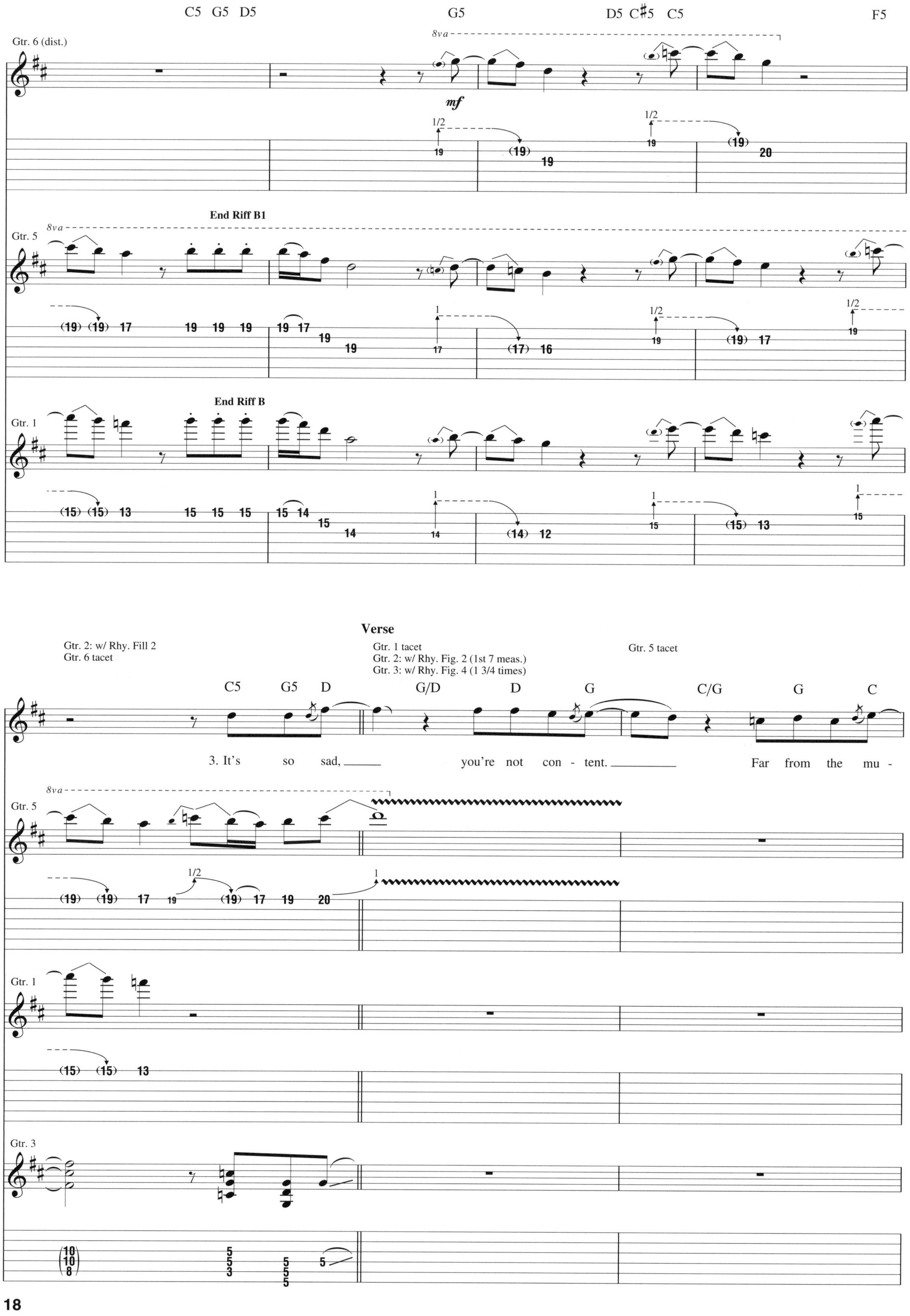
C5 G5 D5
G5
D5 C#5 C5
F5
Gr. 6 (dist.)
8va
mf
1/2
Gtr. 5
End Riff B1
1
Gtr. 1
End Riff B
Verse
Gtr. 2: w/ Rhy. Fill 2
Gtr. 6 tacet
Gtr. 1 tacet
Gtr. 2: w/ Rhy. Fig. 2 (1st 7 meas.)
Gtr. 3: w/ Rhy. Fig. 4 (1 3/4 times)
Gtr. 5 tacet
C5 G5 D
G/D D G
C/G G C
3. It's so sad, you're not con - tent. Far from the mu -
Gtr. 3

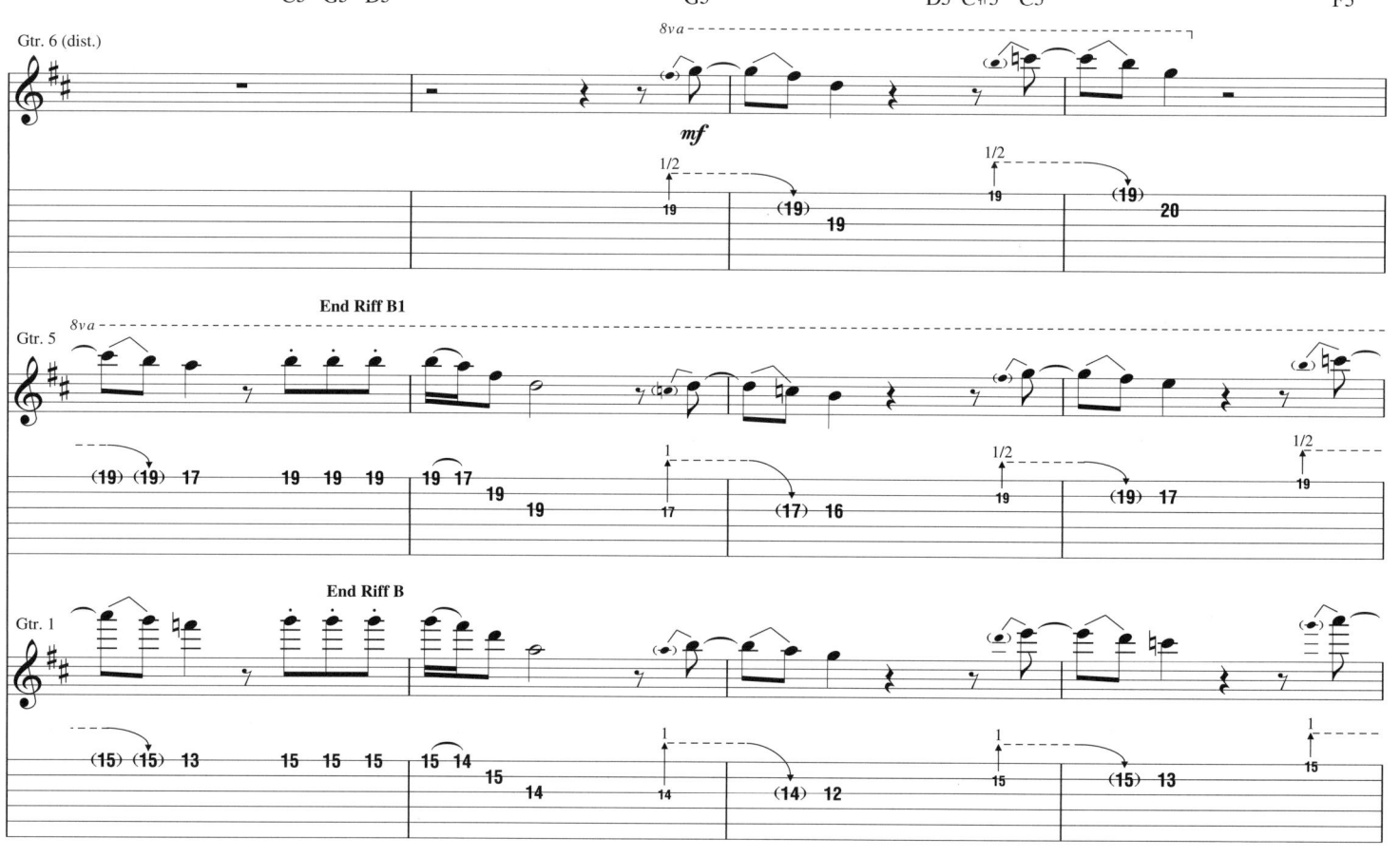

F/C C F C/E F C D G/D D G
- sic and the ne - on glow. Ain't you glad we got the time?
Gtrs. 2 & 3: w/ Rhy. Fill 3
C/G G C F/C C F C/E F C
Far from our folks, they'll nev - er, ev - er know. I'm the king
Bridge
Half-time feel
D5 G5 C5 F5
Rhy. Fig. 5
End Rhy. Fig. 5
Gtr. 2
of the night time world, and you're my head-line queen. I'm the king
Riff C1
End Riff C1
Gtr. 6
mp
Riff C
End Riff C
Gtr. 5
mp
Rhy. Fig. 5A
End Rhy. Fig. 5A
Gtr. 3
Rhy. Fill 3
Gtrs. 2 & 3

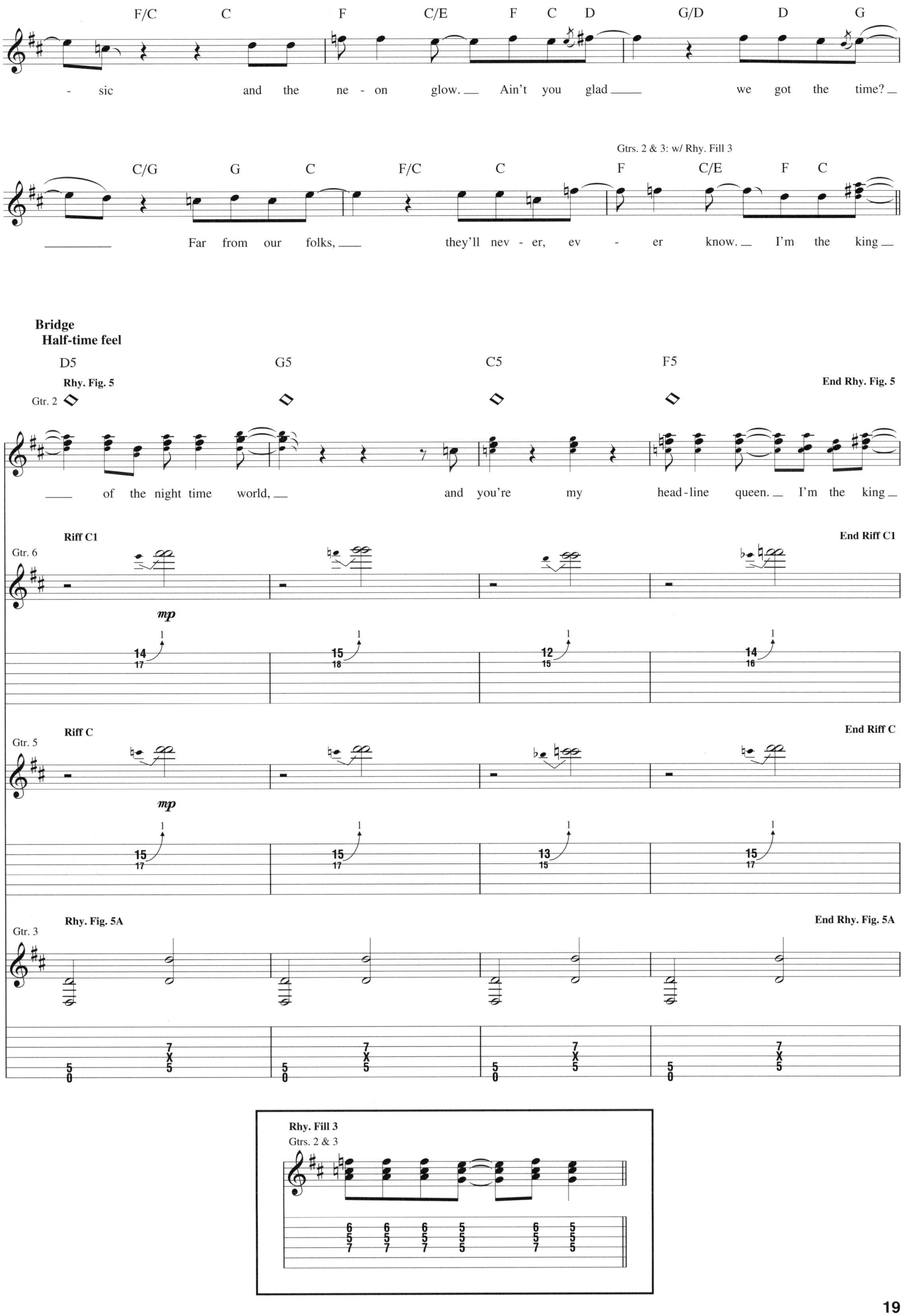

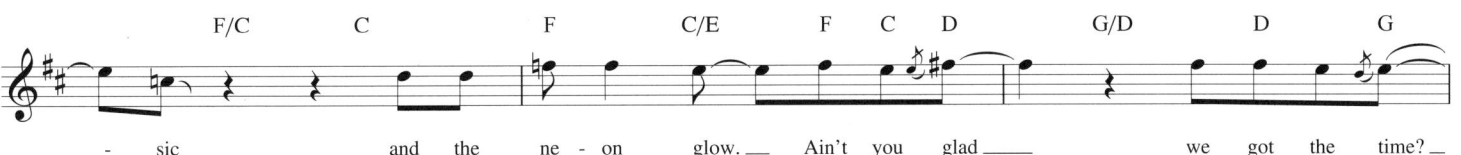

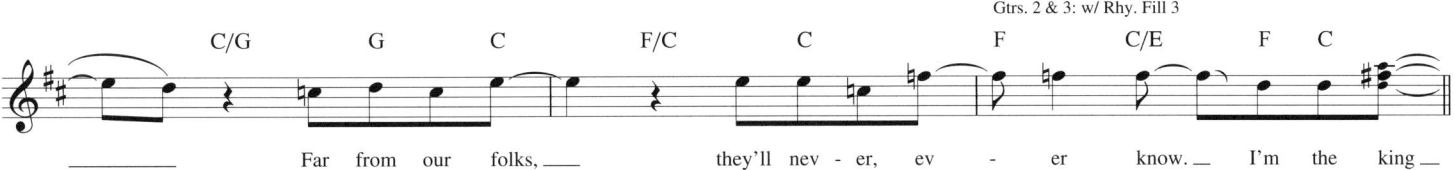

End half-time feel
Gtrs. 2 & 3: w/ Rhy. Figs. 5 & 5A (2 times)
Gtrs. 5 & 6: w/ Riffs C & C1
D5 G5/D C5/D F5/D
of the night time world, come live your se - cret dream. I'm the king,
Gtr. 1
15 15 15 15
Gtr. 1: w/ Riff B (2 times)
D5 G5/D C5/D F5/D
I'm the king, I'm the king, I'm the king, I'm the king
D5 G5 C5 F5 C5 G5 D5
Gtr. 1
I'm the king, I'm the king, I'm the king, I'm the king
Gtr. 5
8va
19 19 19
Gtr. 3
7 X 5 5 0
Outro-Chorus
Gtrs. 2 & 3: w/ Rhy. Fig. 3 (till fade)
Gtrs. 1 & 5: w/ Riffs B & B1 (till fade)
G5 D5 C♯5 C5 F5 C5 G5 D5
of the night time world and you're my head-line queen. I'm the king
Play 3 times and fade
G5 D5 C♯5 C5 F5 C5 G5 D5
of the night time world, come live your se - cret dream. I'm the king

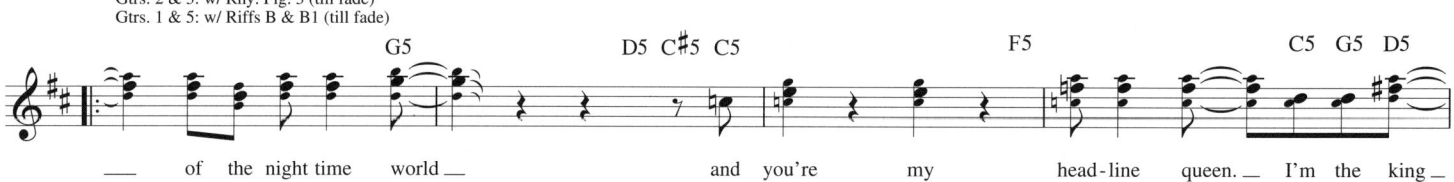

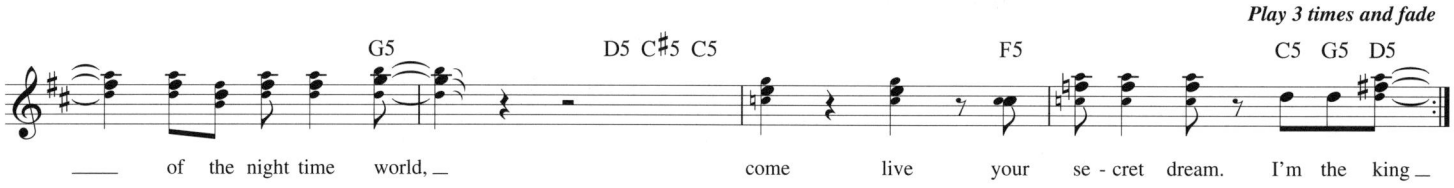

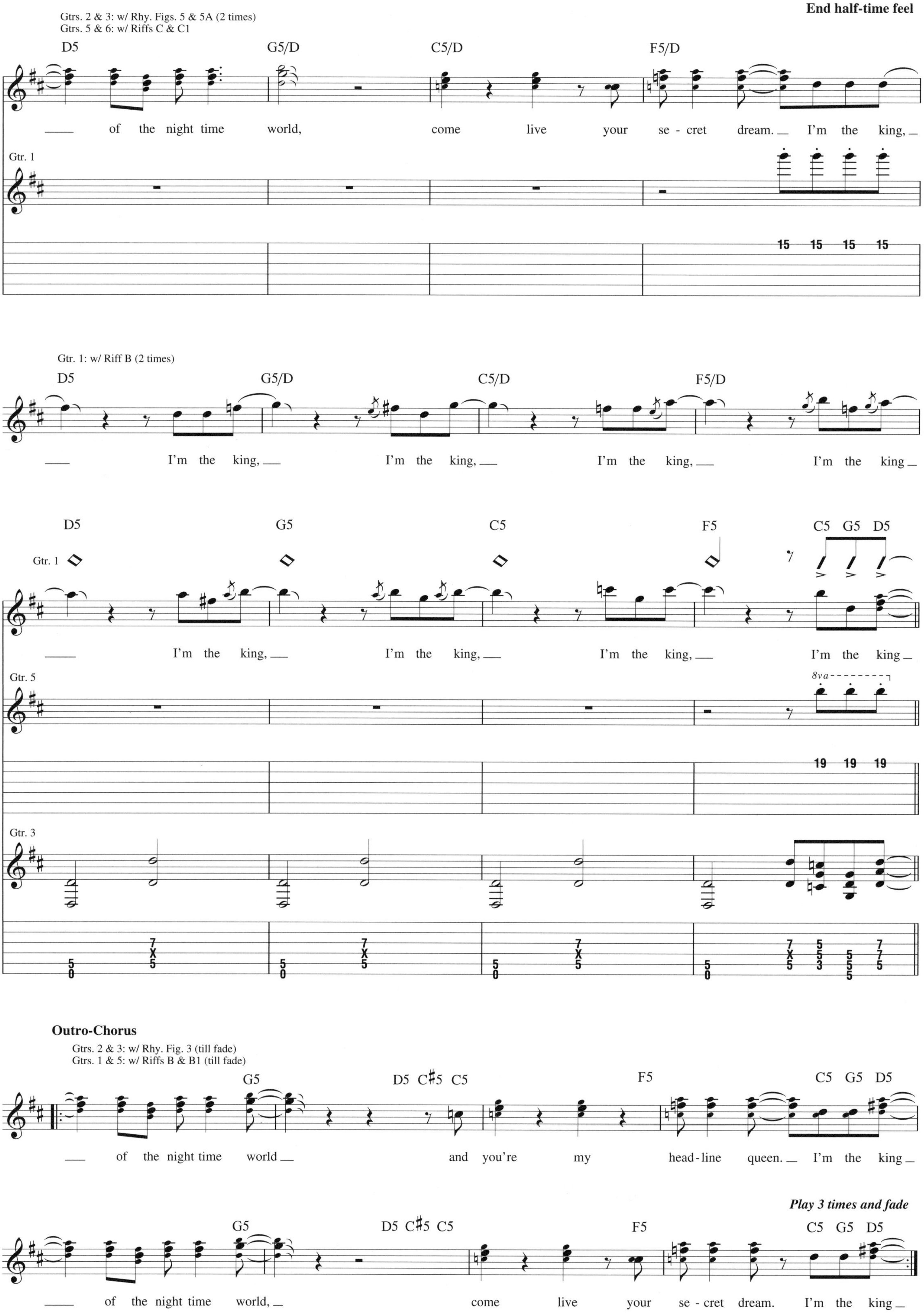

God of Thunder

Words and Music by Paul Stanley

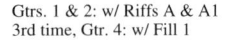

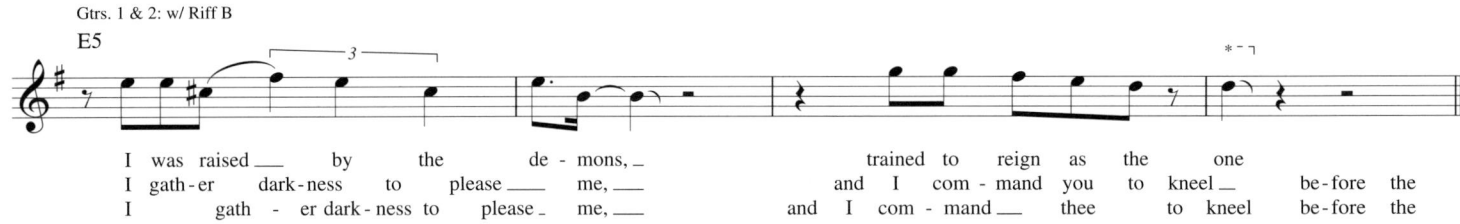

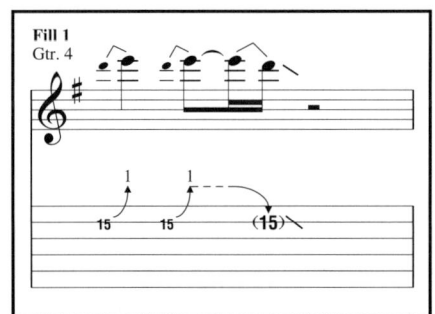

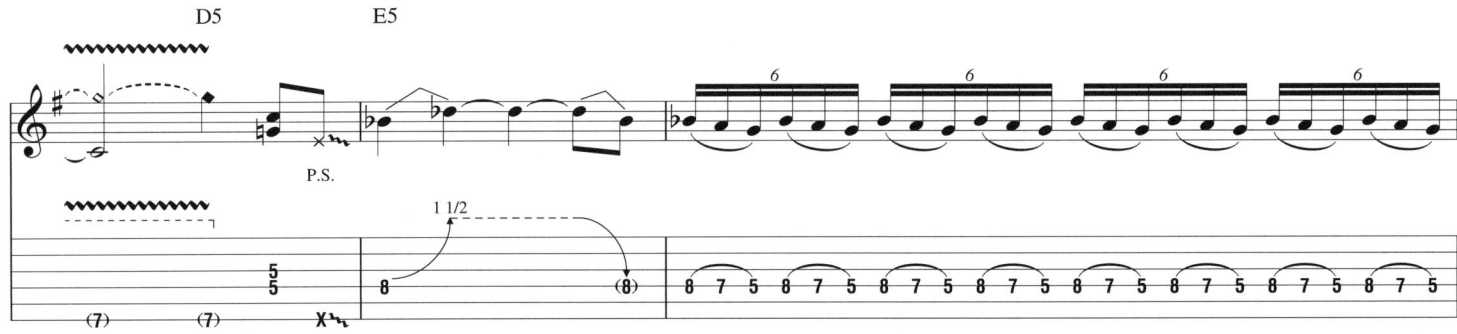
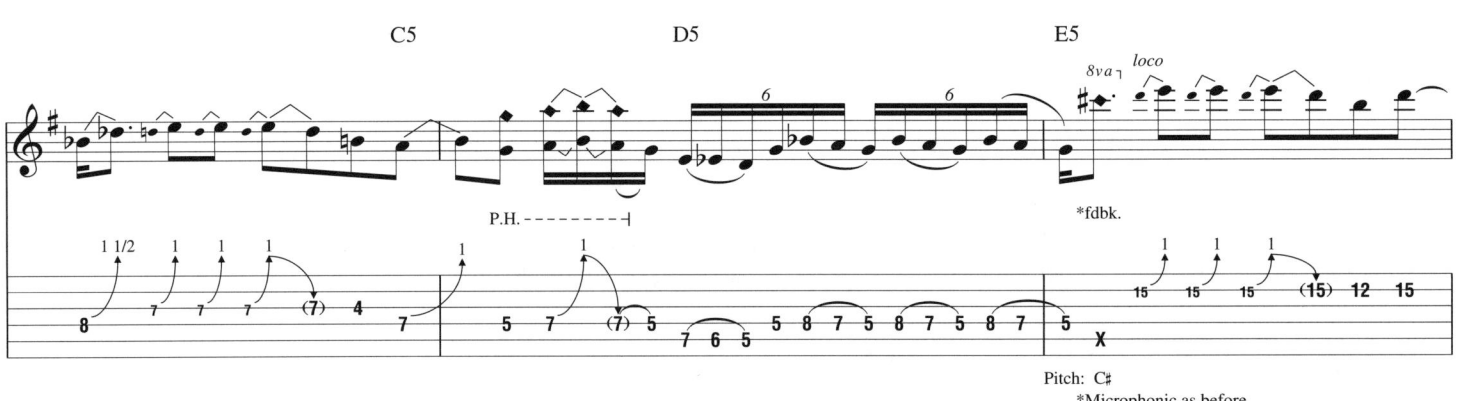
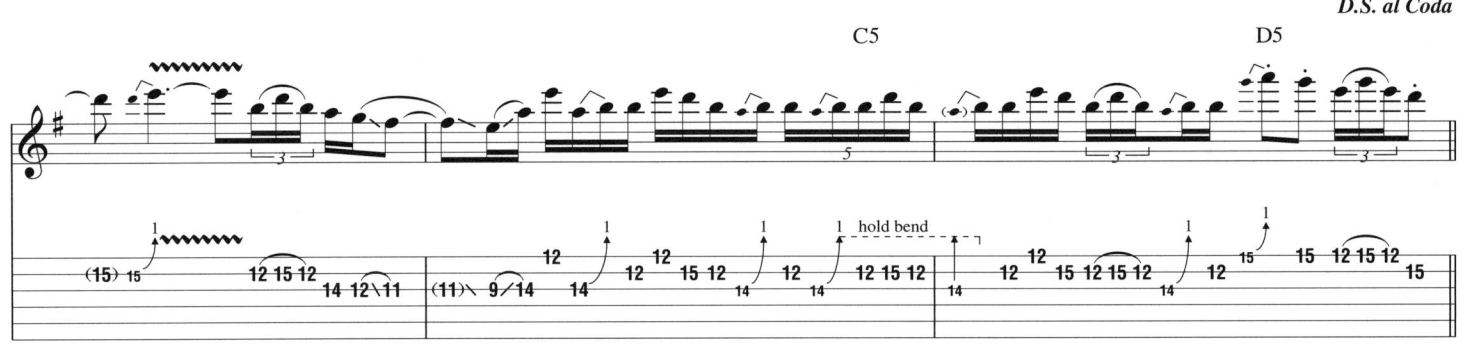

D.S. al Coda

Coda
Outro
Gtrs. 1 & 2: w/ Riffs A & A1 (3 times)

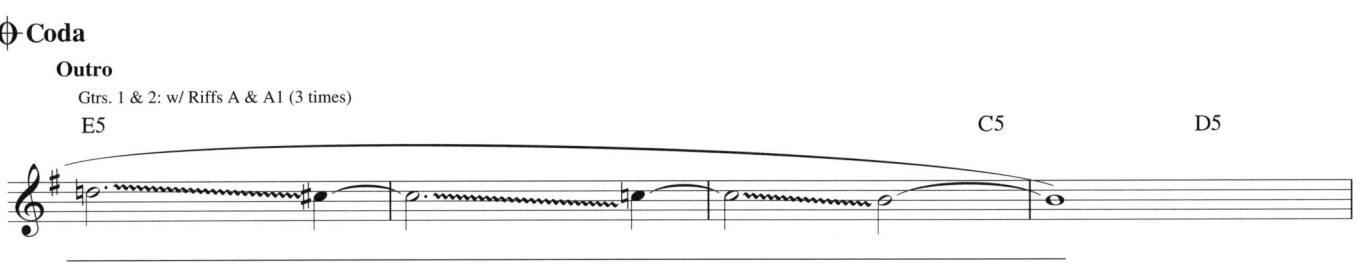

Great Expectations

Words and Music by Gene Simmons and Bob Ezrin

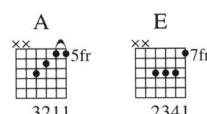

Tune down 1/2 step:
(low to high) E♭-A♭-D♭-G♭-B♭-E♭

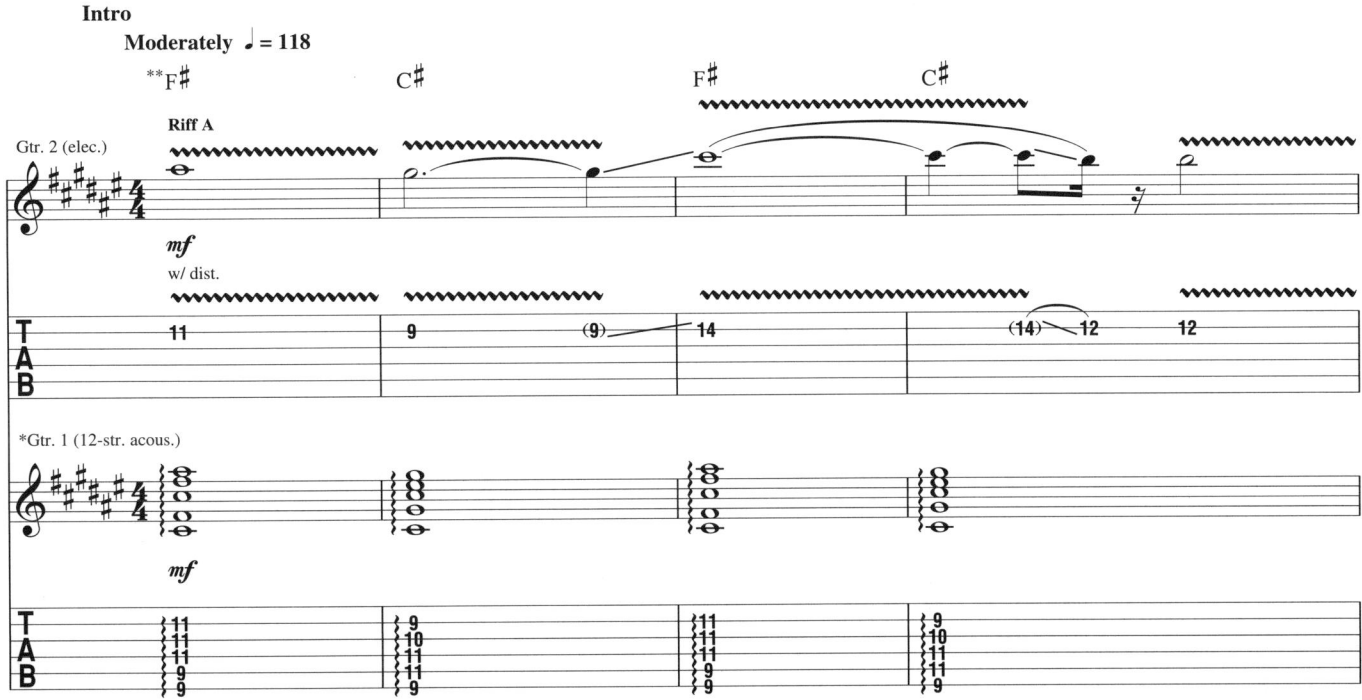

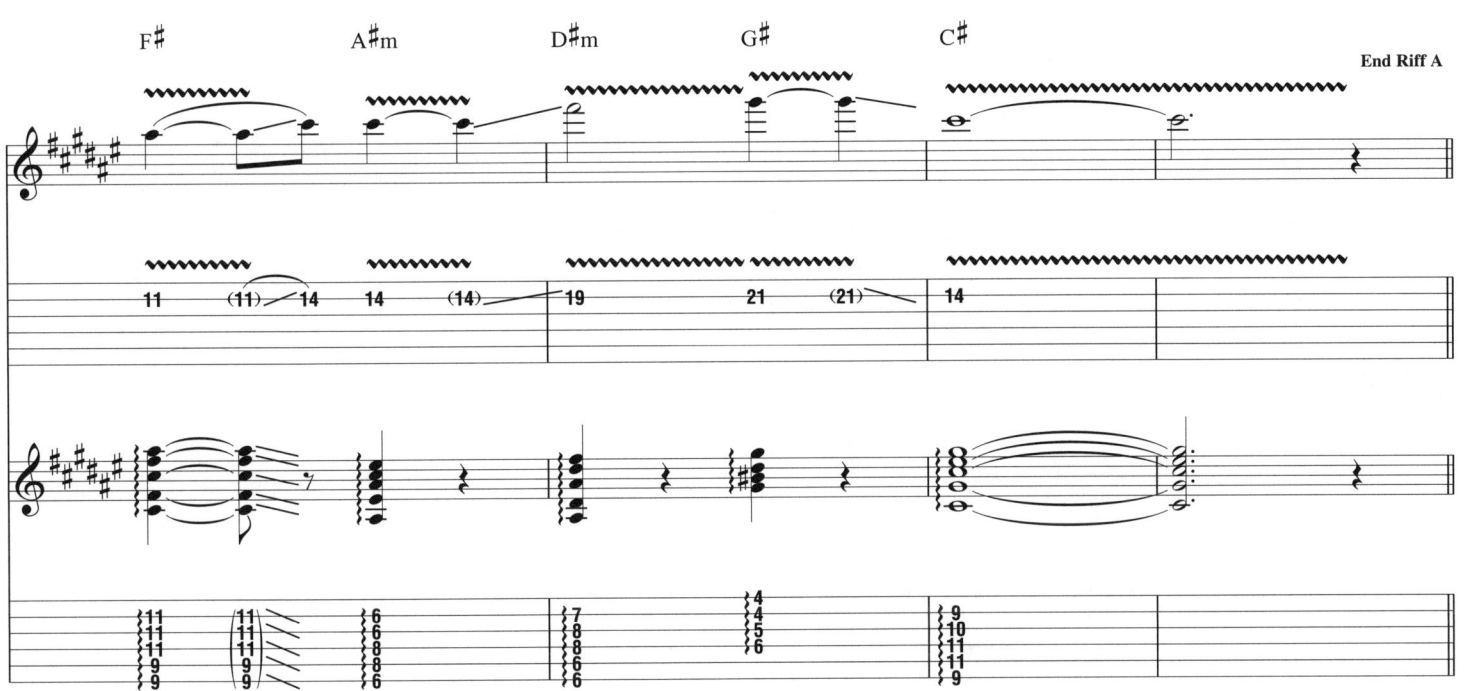

Copyright © 1976 HORI PRODUCTIONS AMERICA, INC., ALL BY MYSELF MUSIC and CAFE AMERICANA
Copyright Renewed
All Rights for HORI PRODUCTIONS AMERICA, INC. and ALL BY MYSELF MUSIC Controlled and Administered by
UNIVERSAL - POLYGRAM INTERNATIONAL PUBLISHING, INC.
All Rights for CAFE AMERICANA in the U.S. Administered by INTERSONG U.S.A., INC.
All Rights outside the U.S. excluding Japan Controlled and Administered by UNIVERSAL - POLYGRAM INTERNATIONAL PUBLISHING, INC.
All Rights Reserved   Used by Permission

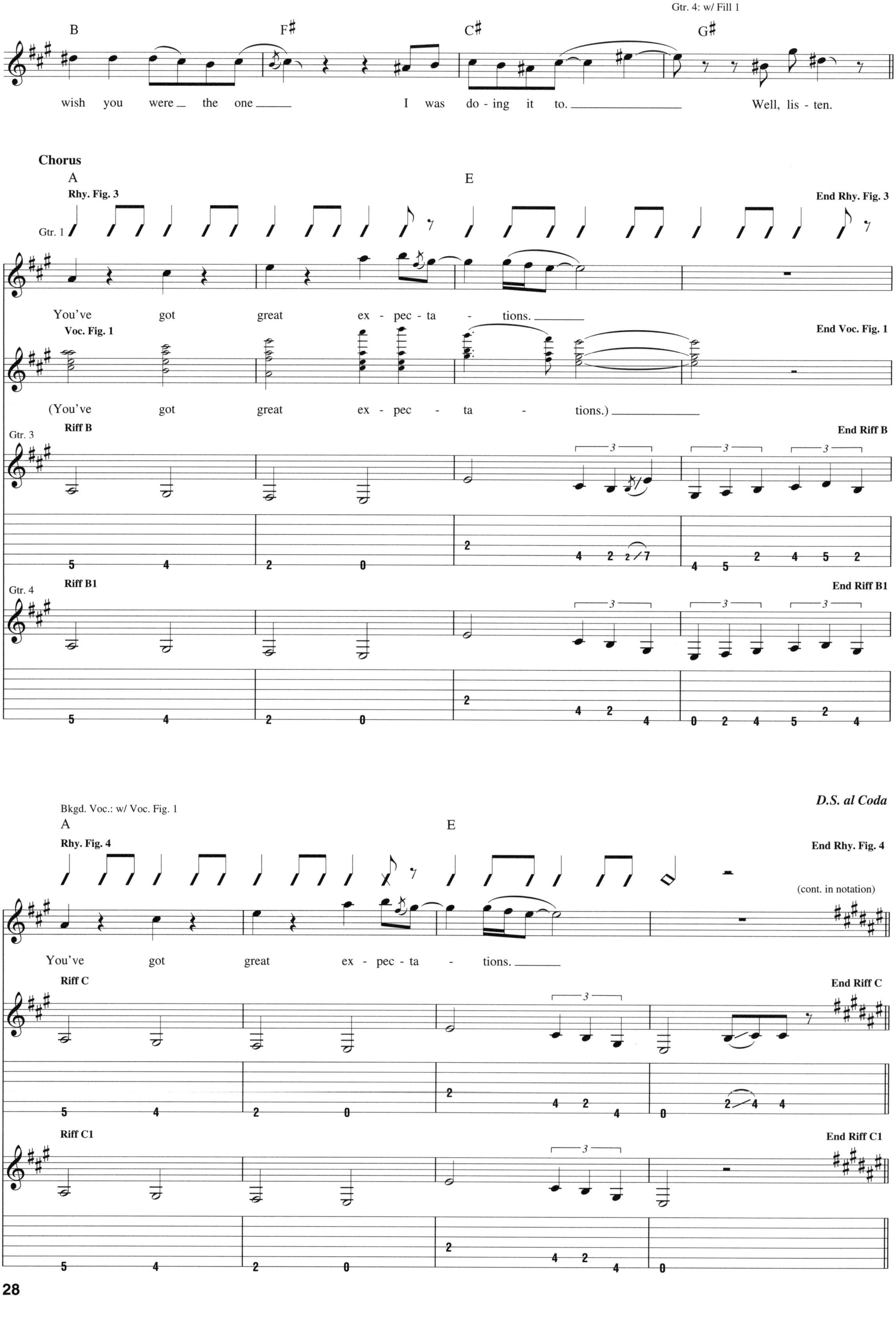
Gtr. 4: w/ Fill 1
B
F♯
C♯
G♯
wish you were the one
I was do - ing it to.
Well, lis - ten.
Chorus
A
E
Rhy. Fig. 3
End Rhy. Fig. 3
Gtr. 1
You've got great ex - pec - ta - tions.
Voc. Fig. 1
End Voc. Fig. 1
(You've got great ex - pec - ta - tions.)
Riff B
End Riff B
Gtr. 3
Gtr. 4
Riff B1
End Riff B1
Bkgd. Voc.: w/ Voc. Fig. 1
D.S. al Coda
Rhy. Fig. 4
End Rhy. Fig. 4
(cont. in notation)
You've got great ex - pec - ta - tions.
Riff C
End Riff C
Riff C1
End Riff C1

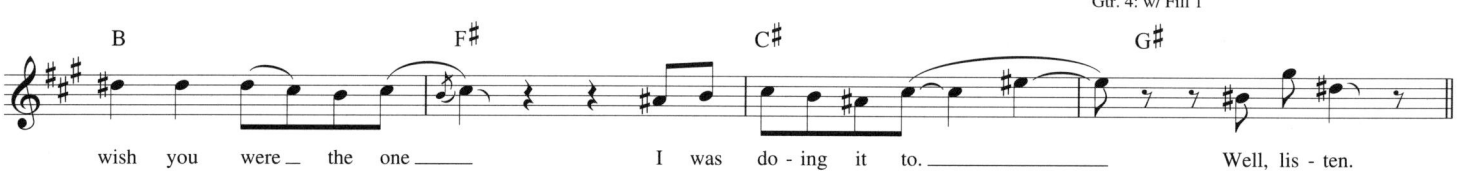

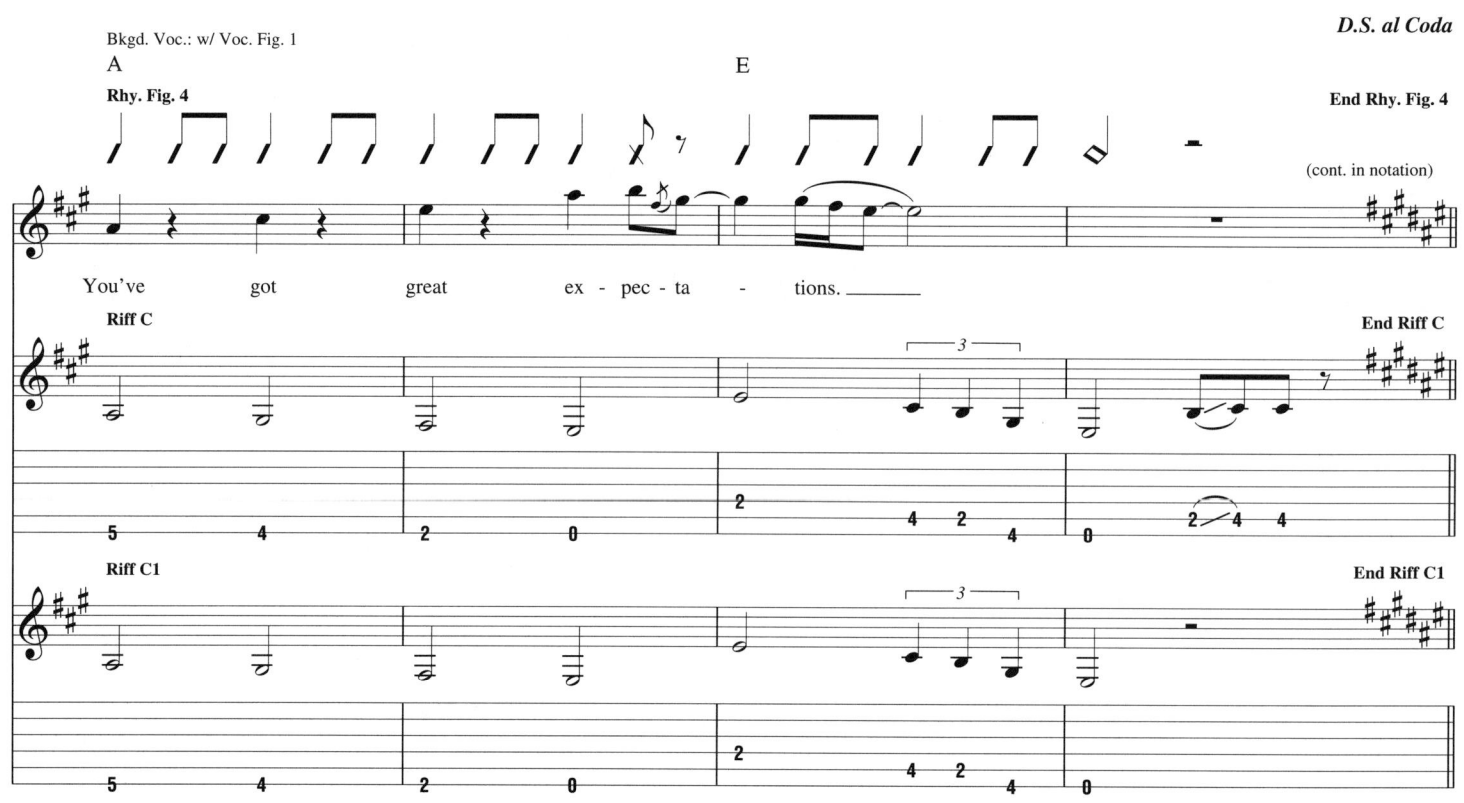

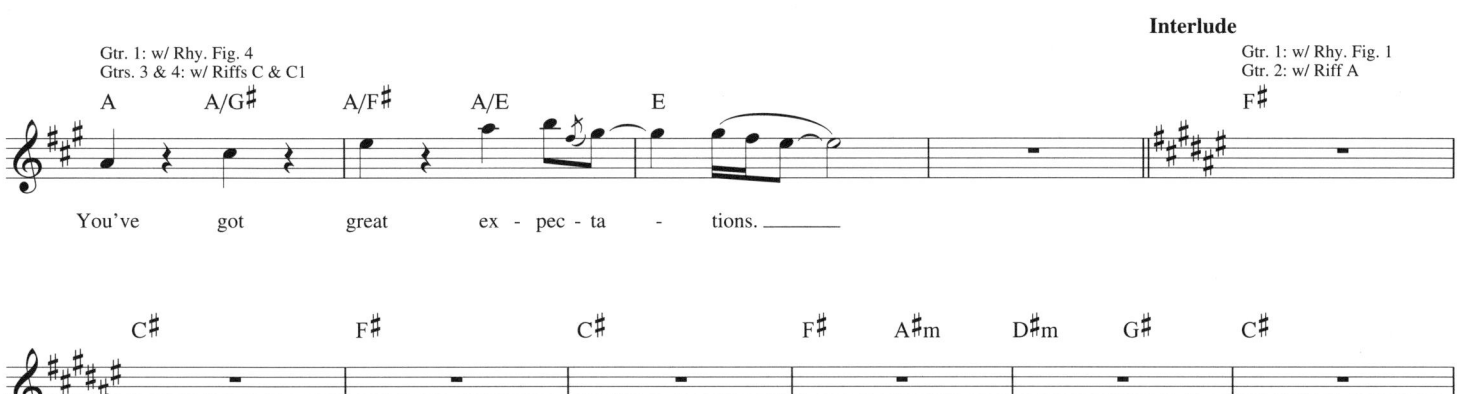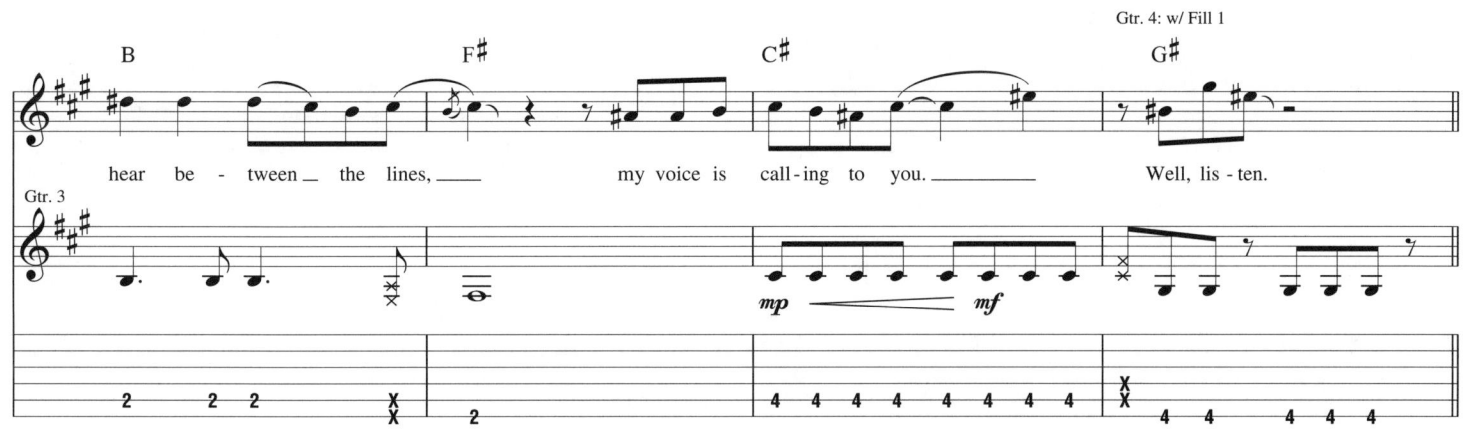

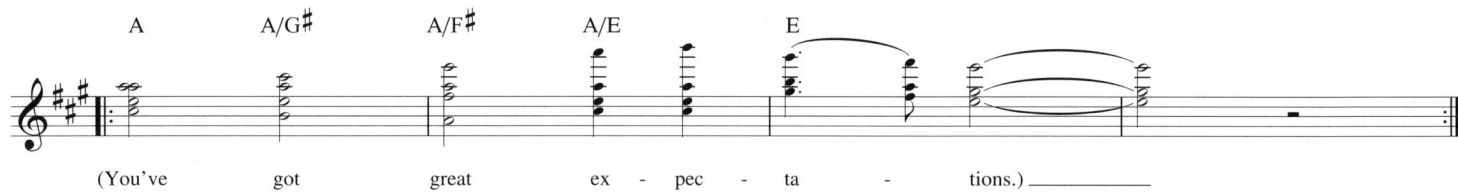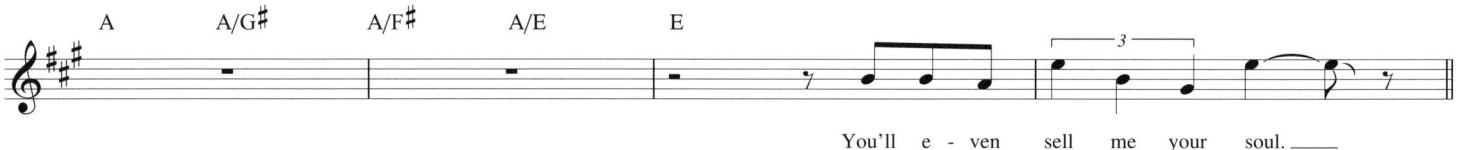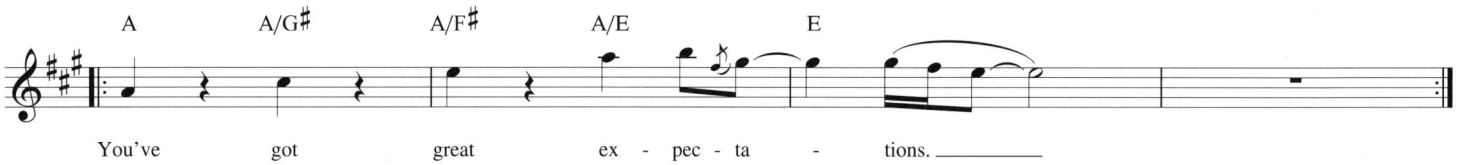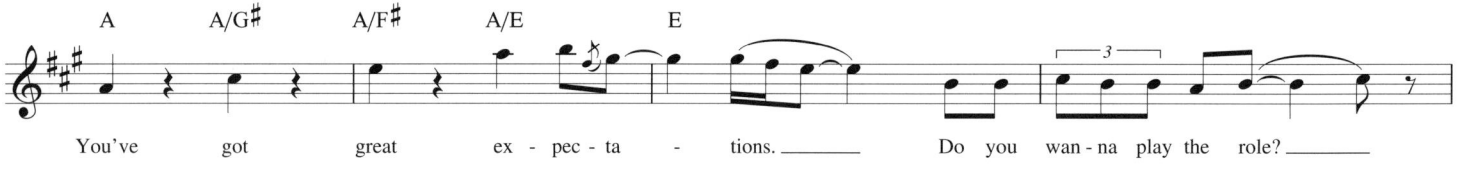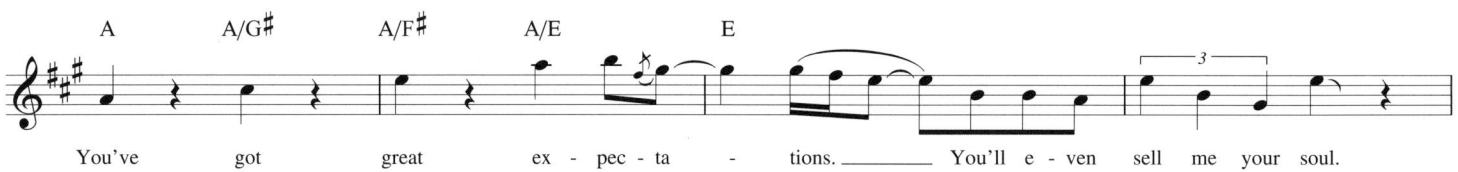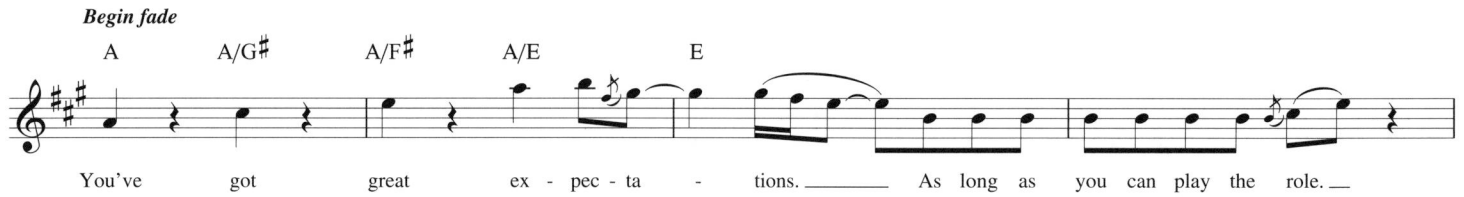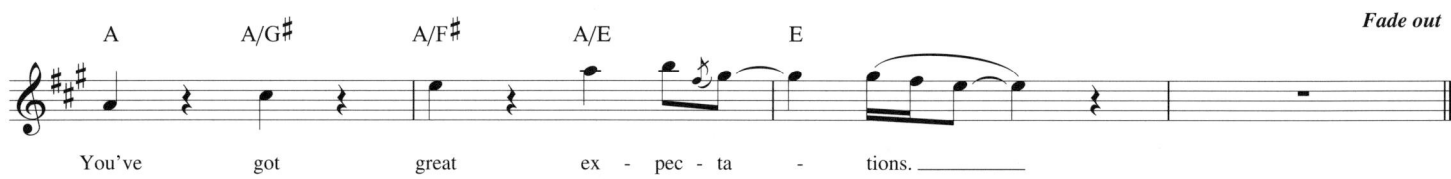

Flaming Youth

Words and Music by Gene Simmons, Paul Stanley, Ace Frehley and Bob Ezrin

Tune down 1/2 step:
(low to high) E♭-A♭-D♭-G♭-B♭-E♭

Intro

Moderate Rock ♩ = 130

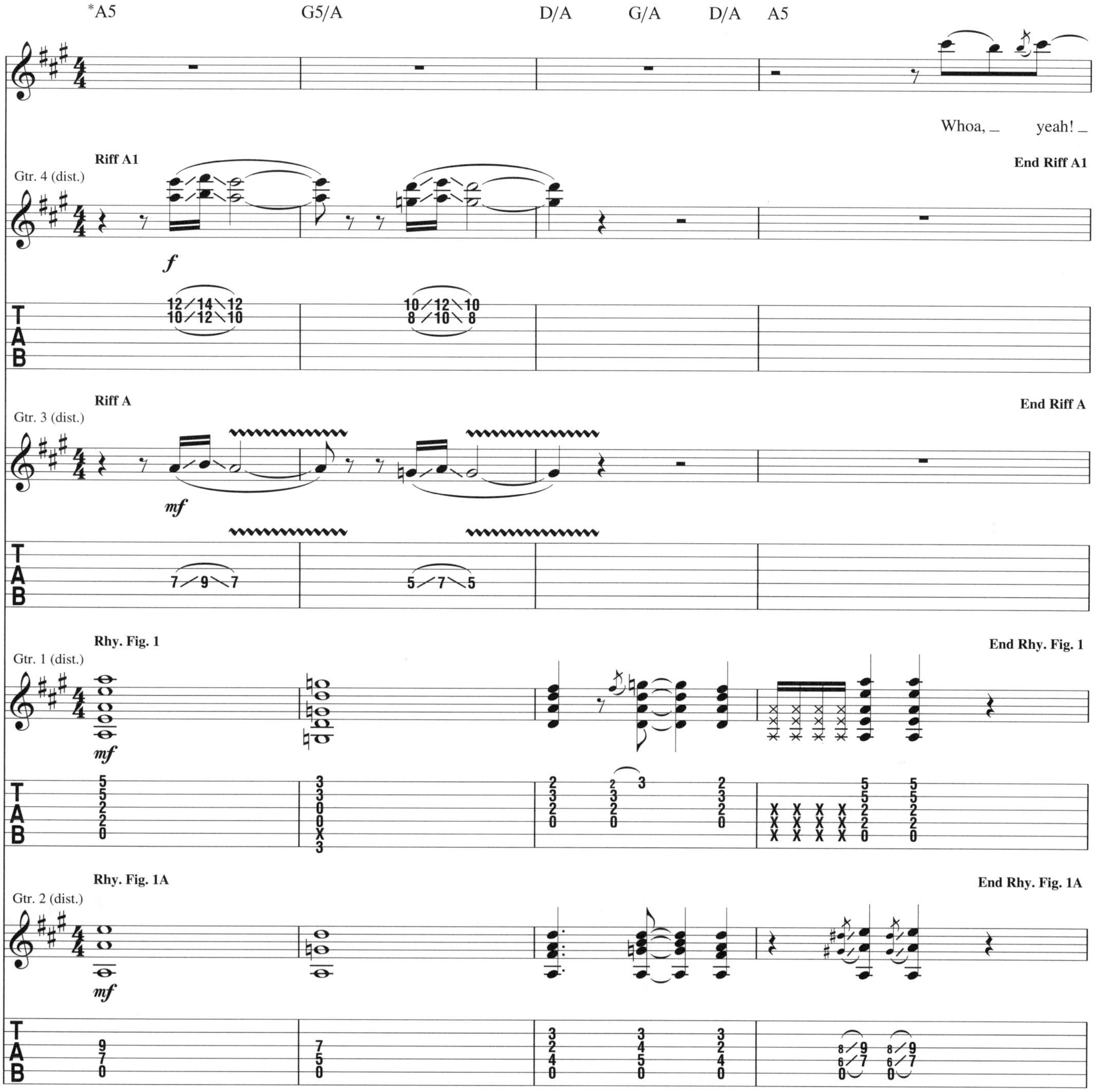

*Chord symbols reflect overall harmony.

Gtrs. 1 & 2: w/ Rhy. Figs. 1 & 1A
Gtrs. 3 & 4: w/ Riffs A & A1

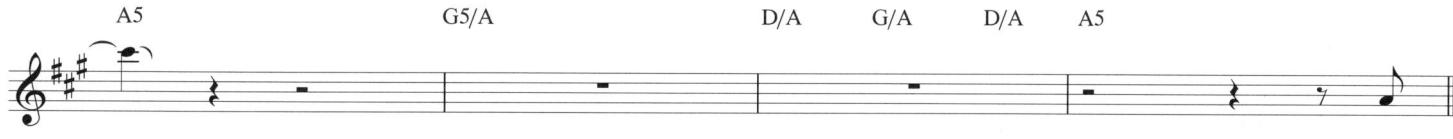

Verse
A5
G5/A
D/A
G/A
D/A
A5
par-ents think _ I'm cra - zy, and they hate the things _ I do. _ I'm
u - ni - form _ is leath - er, and my pow - er is _ my age. _ I'm
Rhy. Fig. 2
End Rhy. Fig. 2
Gtr. 1
Rhy. Fig. 2A
End Rhy. Fig. 2A
Gtr. 2
Gtrs. 1 & 2: w/ Rhy. Figs. 2 & 2A
A5
G5/A
D/A
G/A
D/A
stu - pid and _ I'm la - zy. Man, if they on - ly knew _
get - tin' it _ to - geth - er to break out of _ my cage. _
Chorus
A5
G/D
D
G/D
D
how
'Cause
flam - ing youth _ will set the world _ on fi -
Rhy. Fig. 3B
*Gtr. 3
mf
let ring
let ring
*Organ arr. for gtr.
Gtr. 2
Rhy. Fig. 3A
Gtr. 1
Rhy. Fig. 3

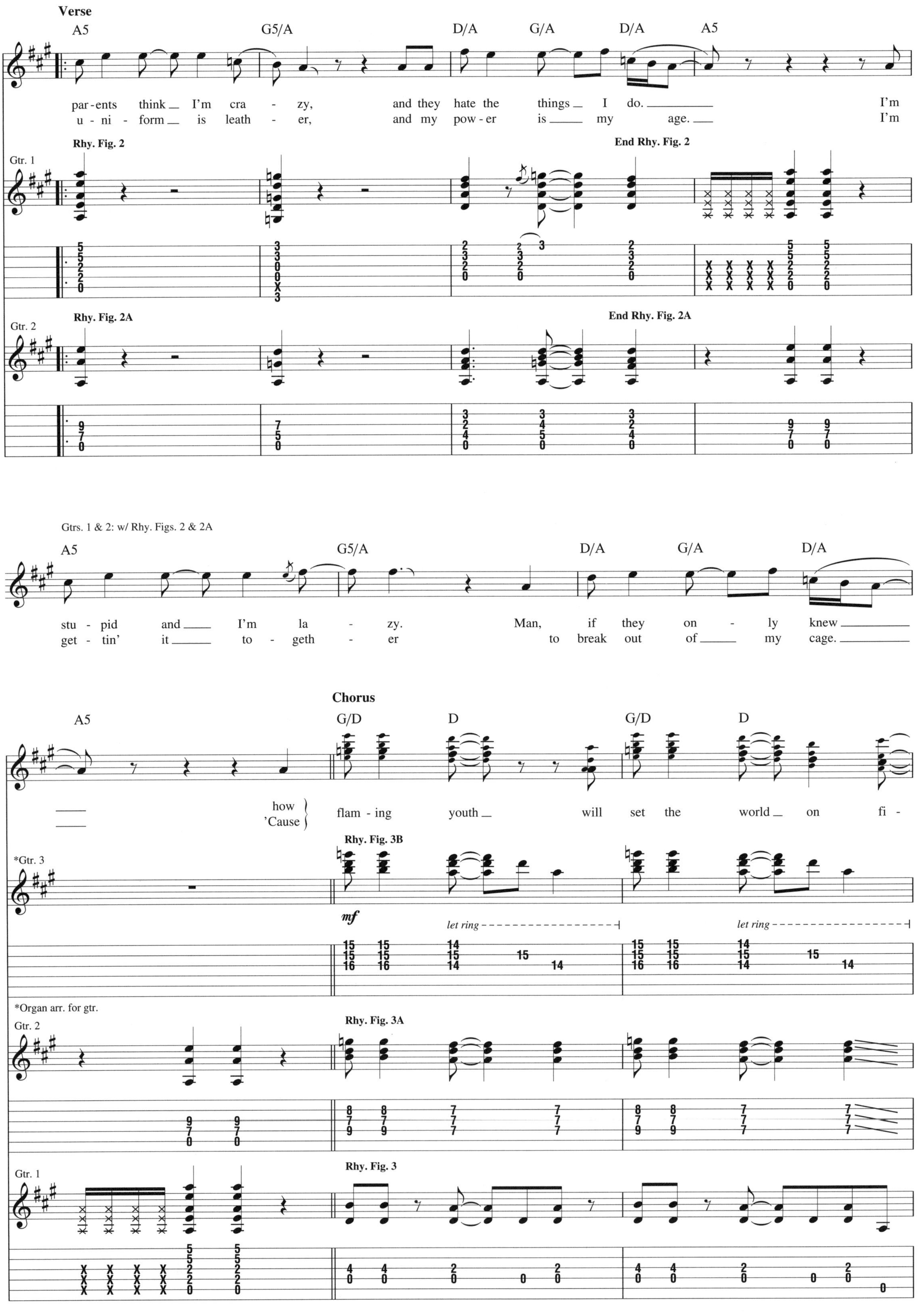

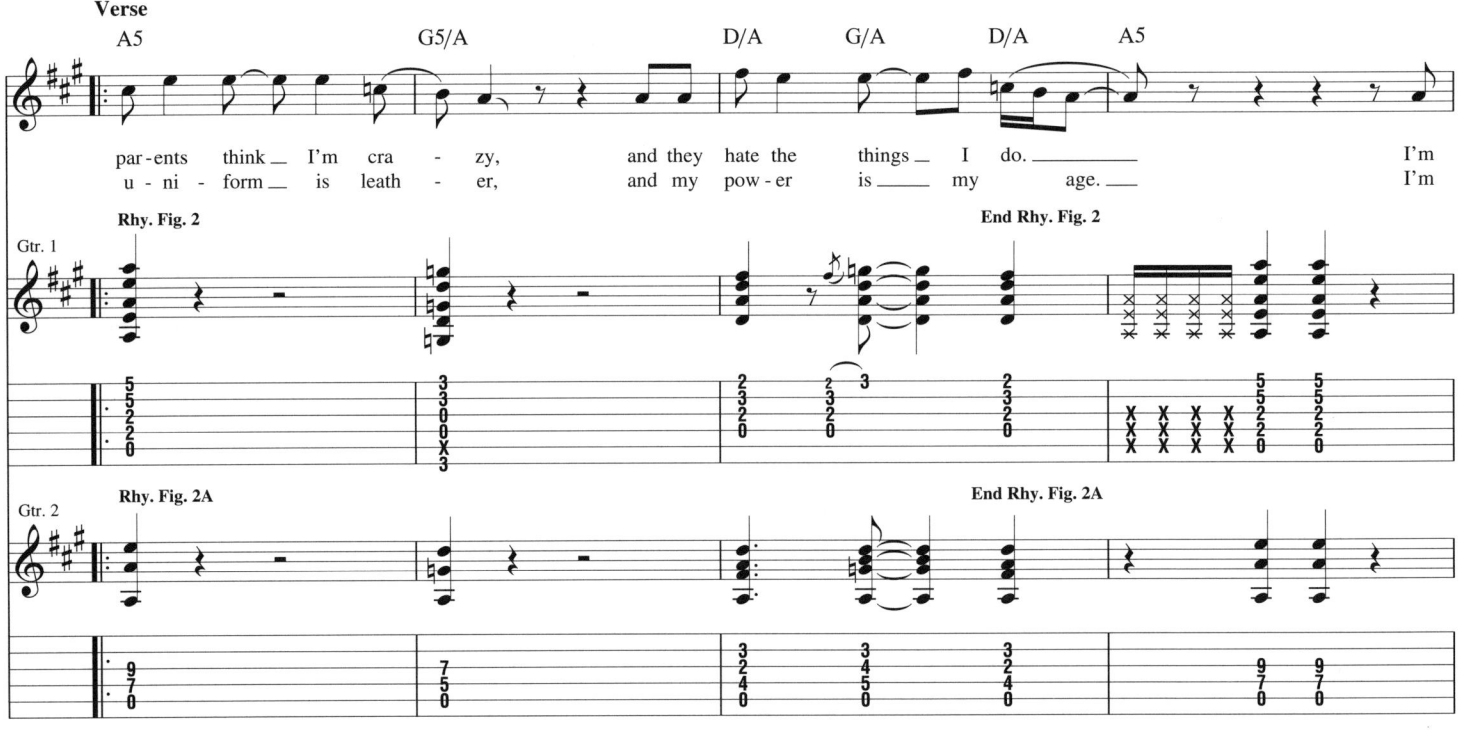

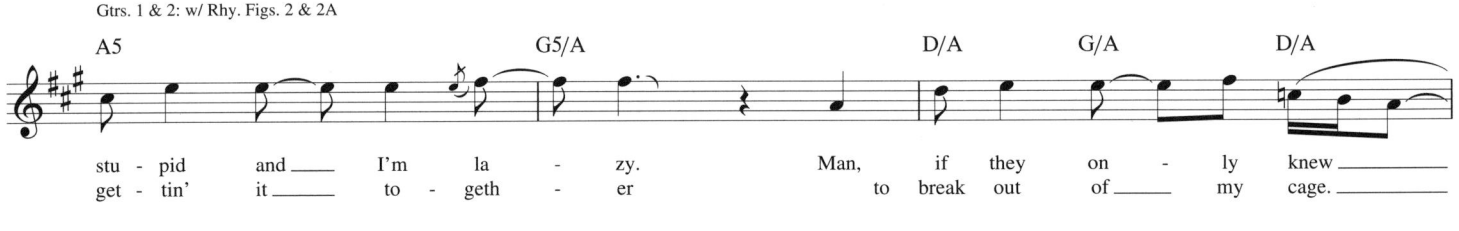

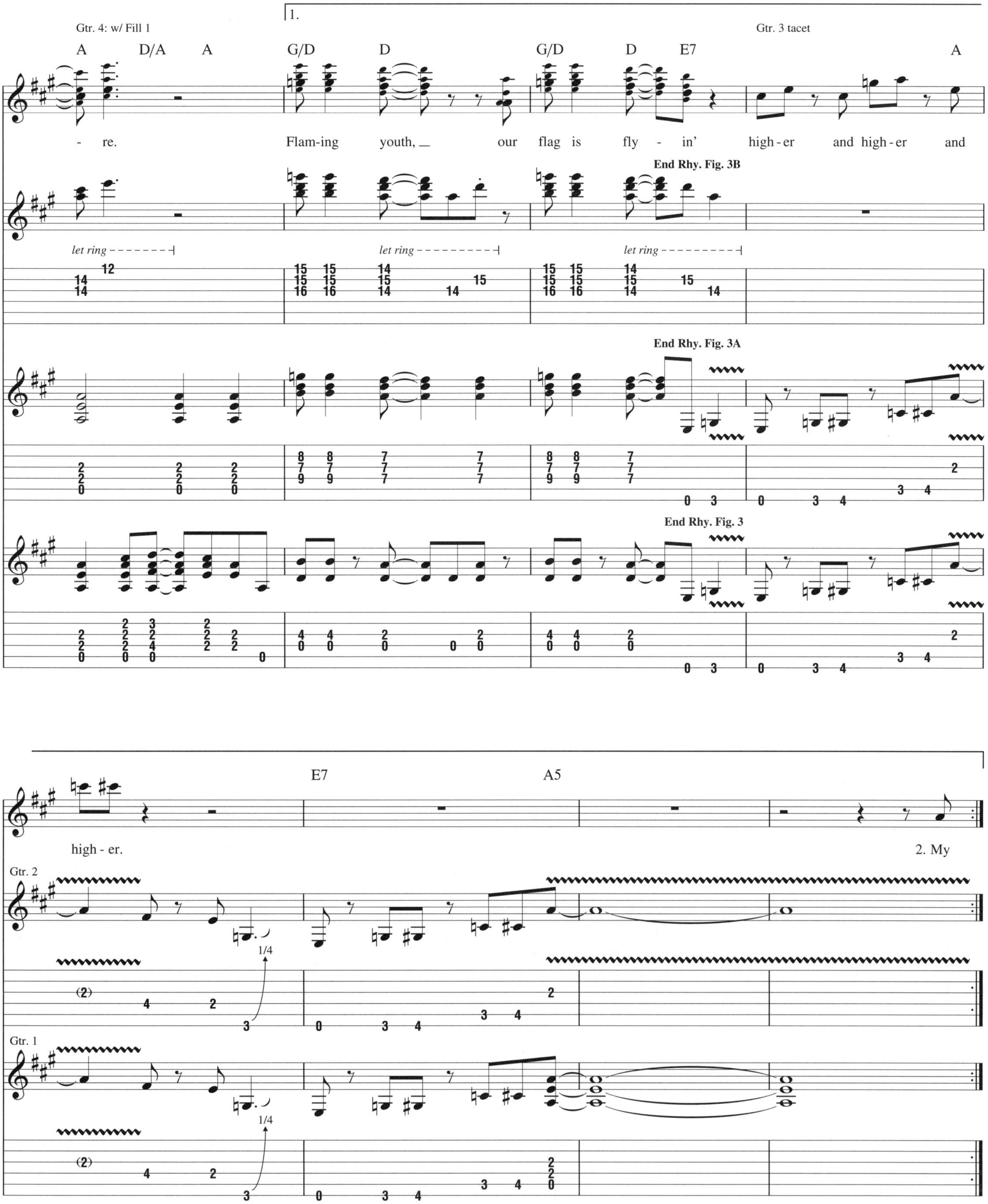
1.
Gtr. 4: w/ Fill 1
Gtr. 3 tacet
A D/A A G/D D G/D D E7 A
- re. Flam-ing youth, _ our flag is fly - in' high-er and high-er and
End Rhy. Fig. 3B
let ring
End Rhy. Fig. 3A
End Rhy. Fig. 3
E7 A5
high - er. 2. My
Gtr. 2
1/4
Gtr. 1
1/4

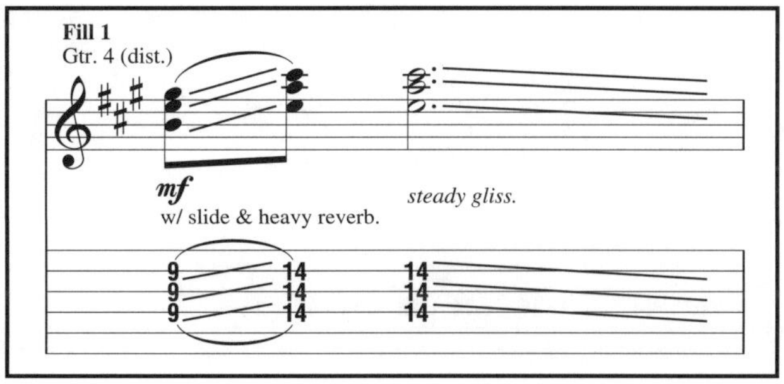
Fill 1
Gtr. 4 (dist.)
mf
w/ slide & heavy reverb.
steady gliss.

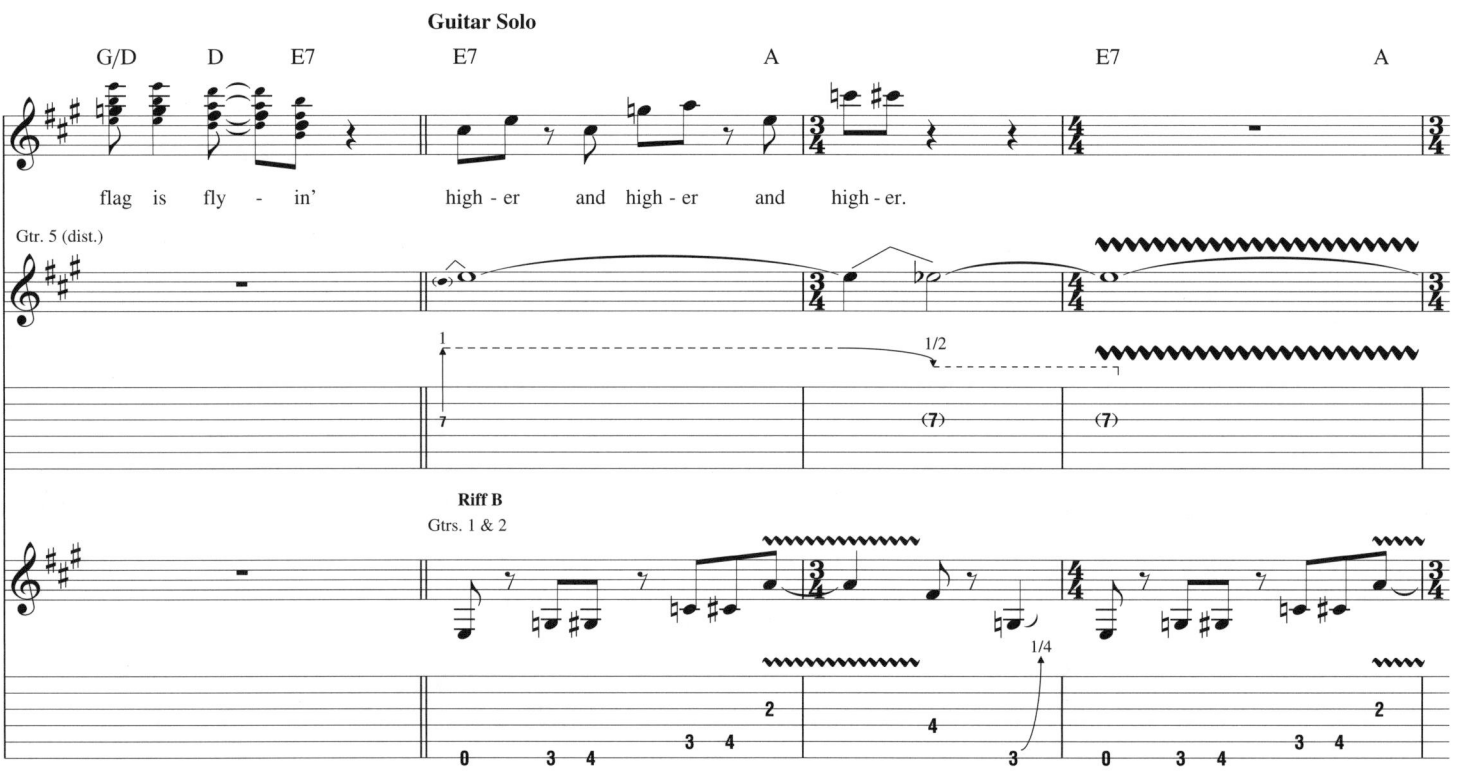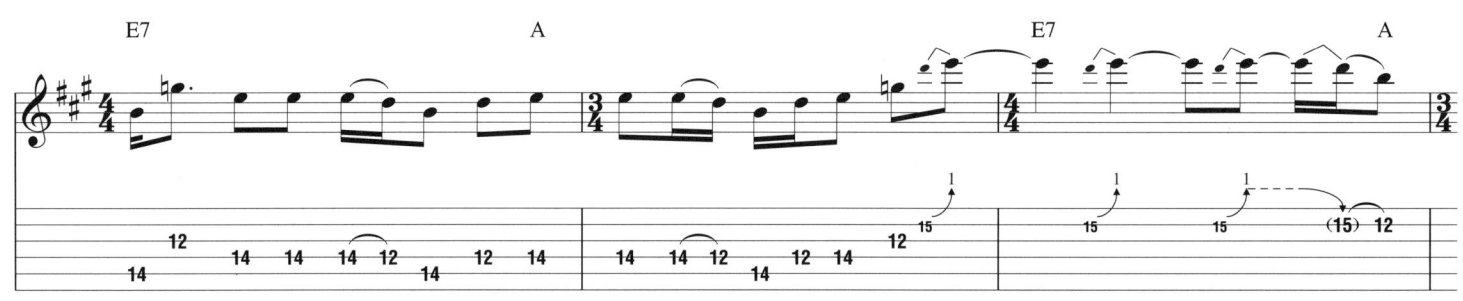

E7
A
E7
A
Gtr. 5
let ring
hold bend
Gtrs. 1 & 2
E7
A5
Gtr. 5
Gtr. 2
fdbk.
Gtr. 1

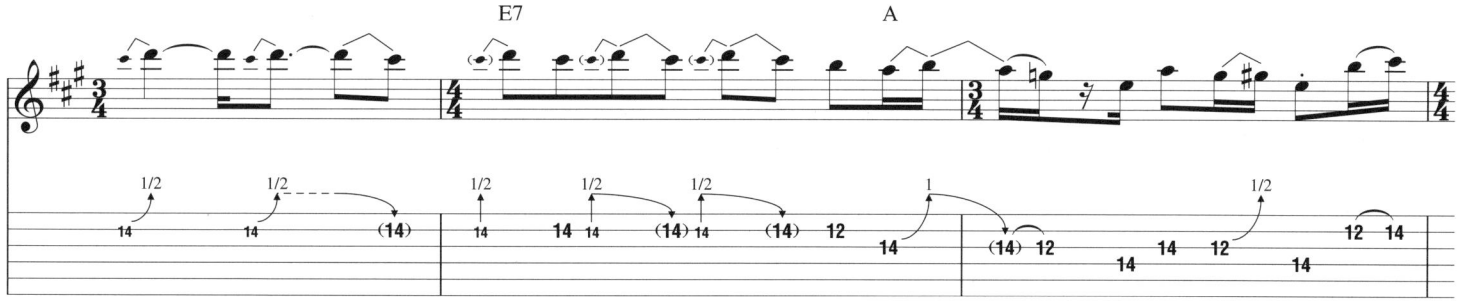

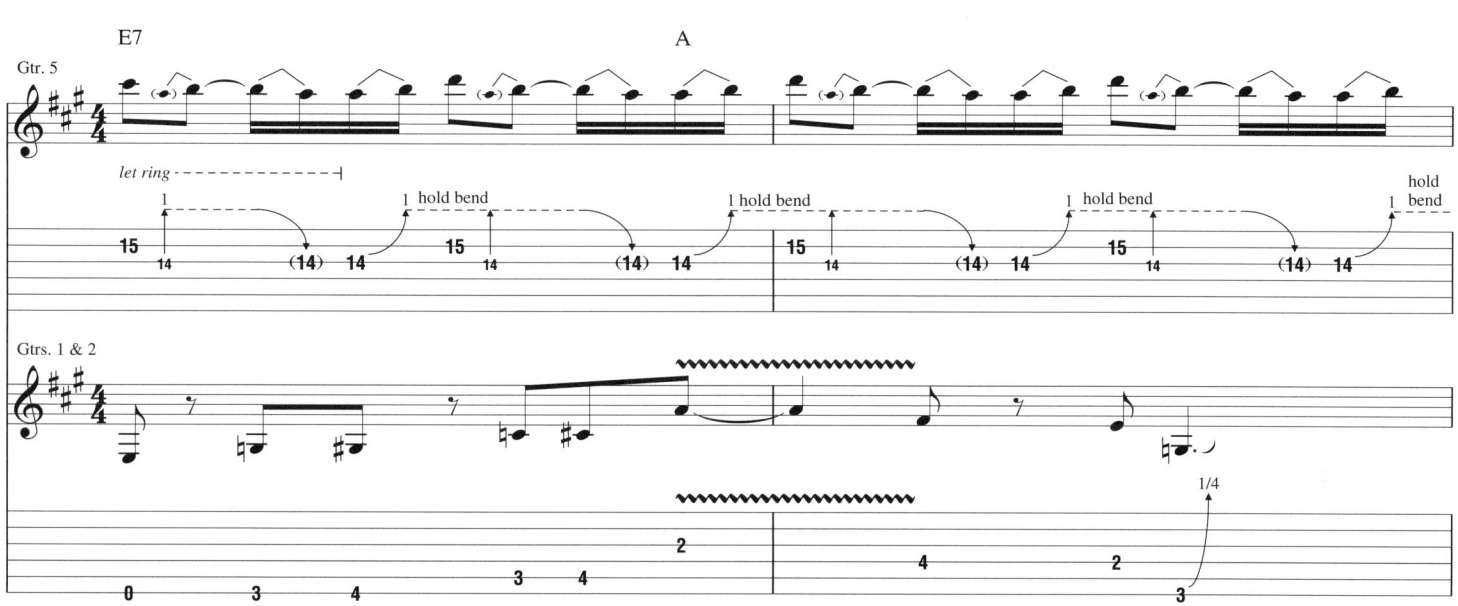

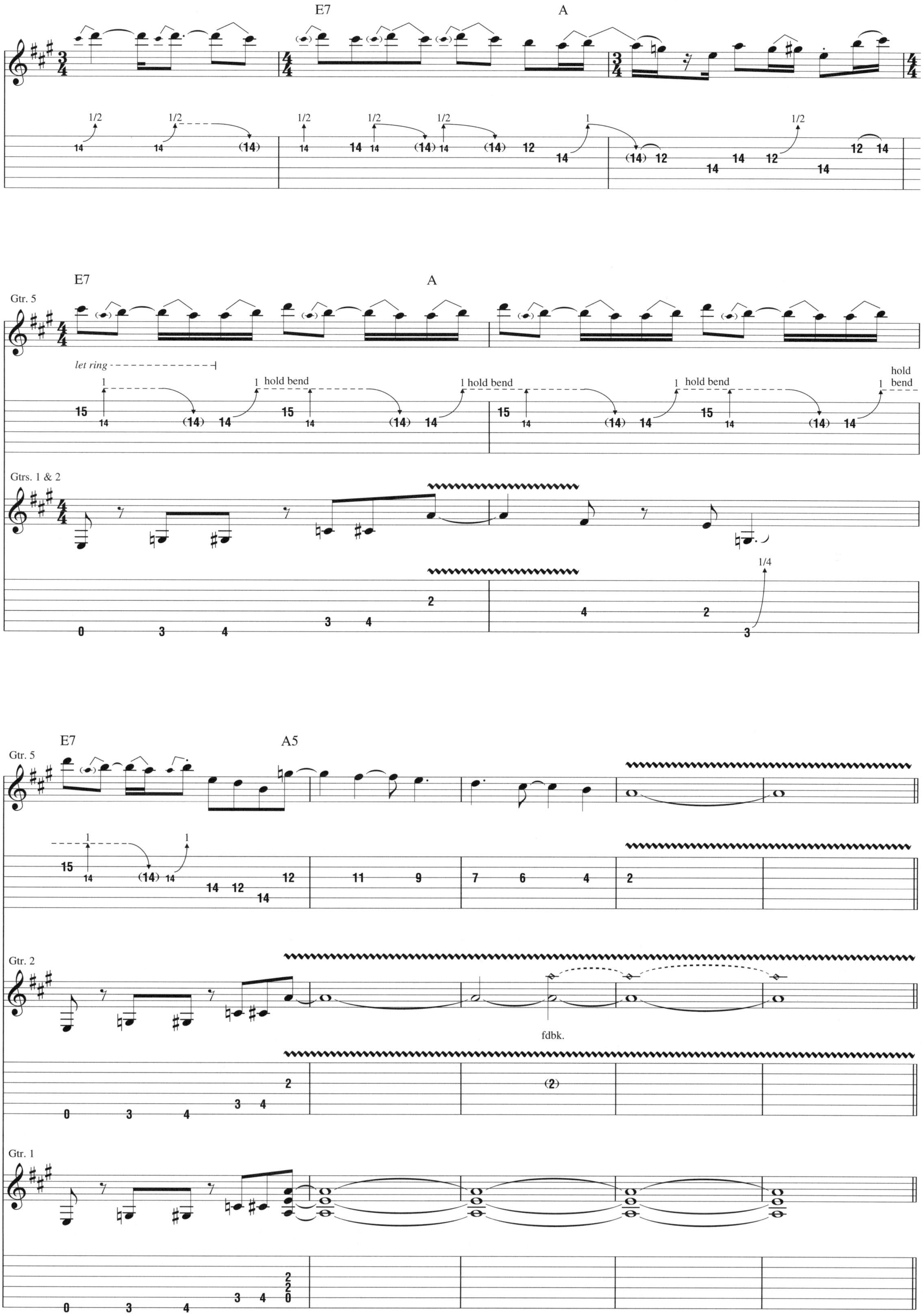

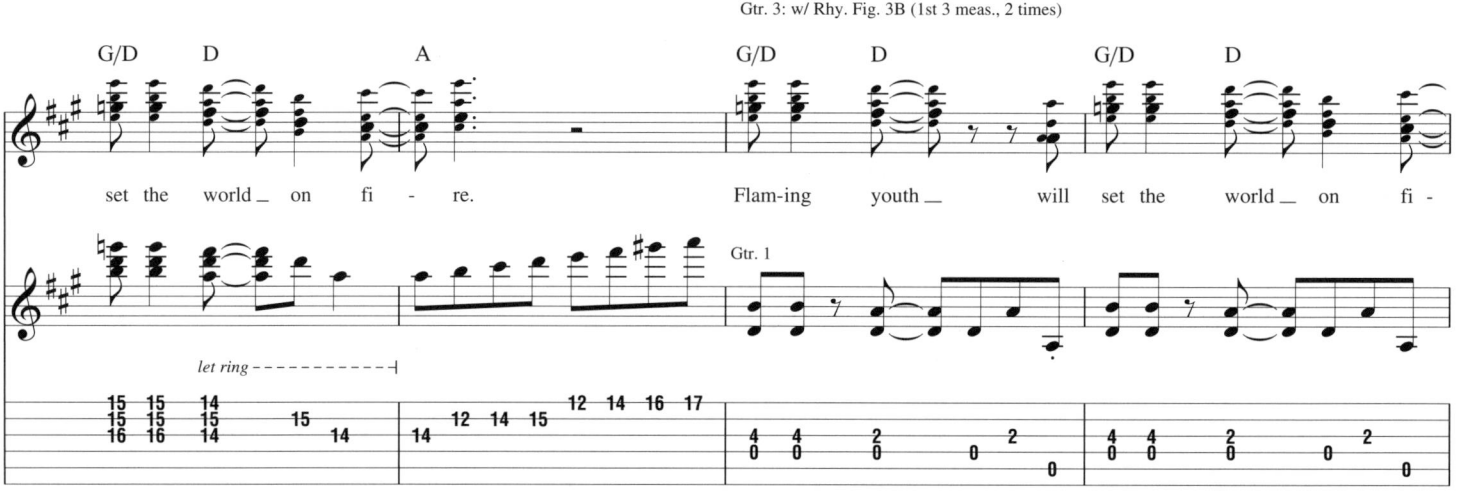
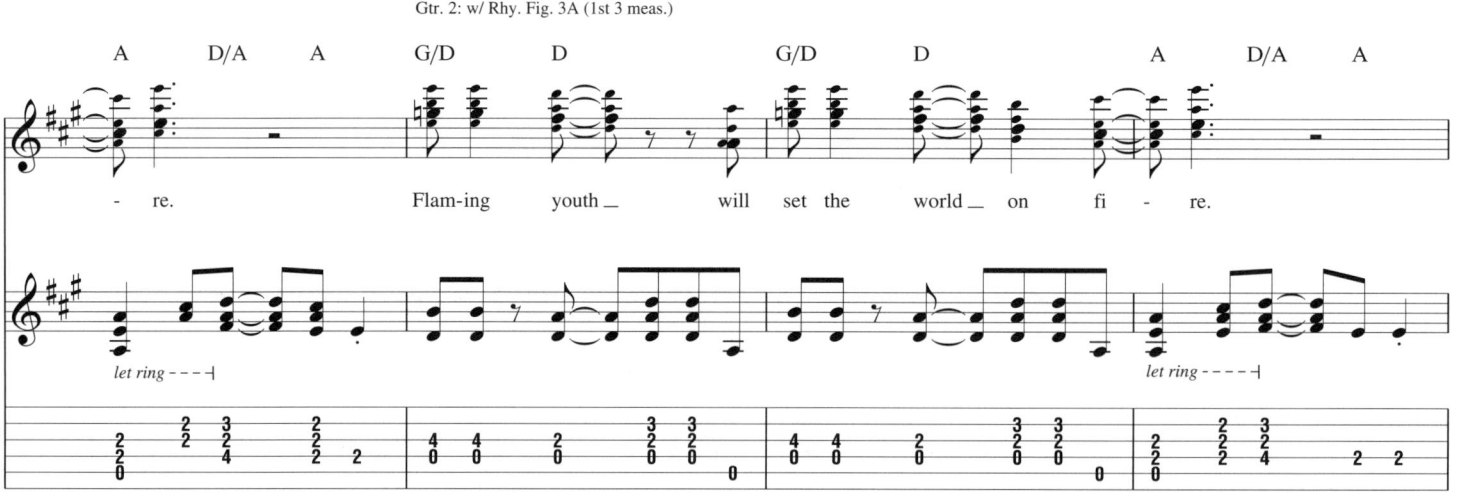

Sweet Pain
Words and Music by Gene Simmons

Tune down 1/2 step:
(low to high) E♭-A♭-D♭-G♭-B♭-E♭

Intro
Moderately ♩ = 130

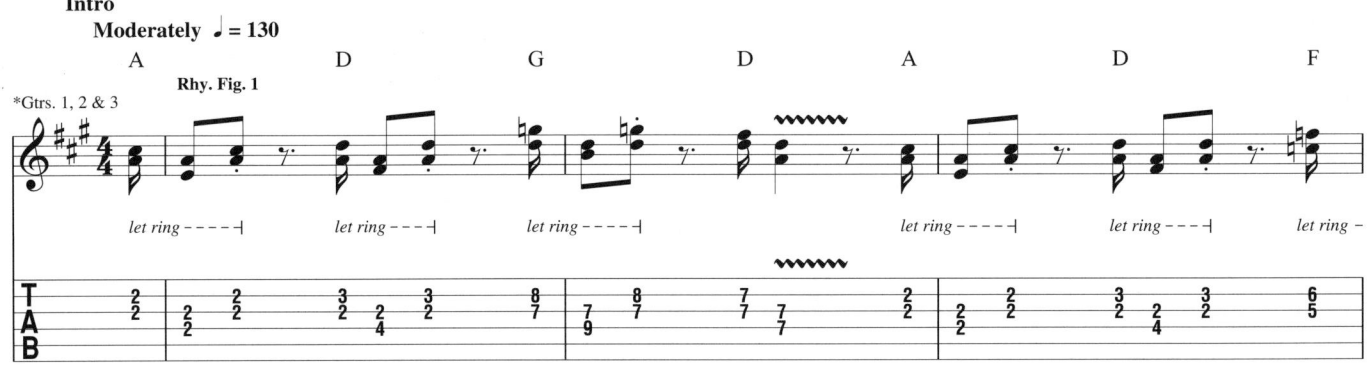

*Gtrs. 1 & 2 (elec.) w/ dist., played *f*;
 Gtr. 3 (acous.), played *mf*.
Composite arrangement

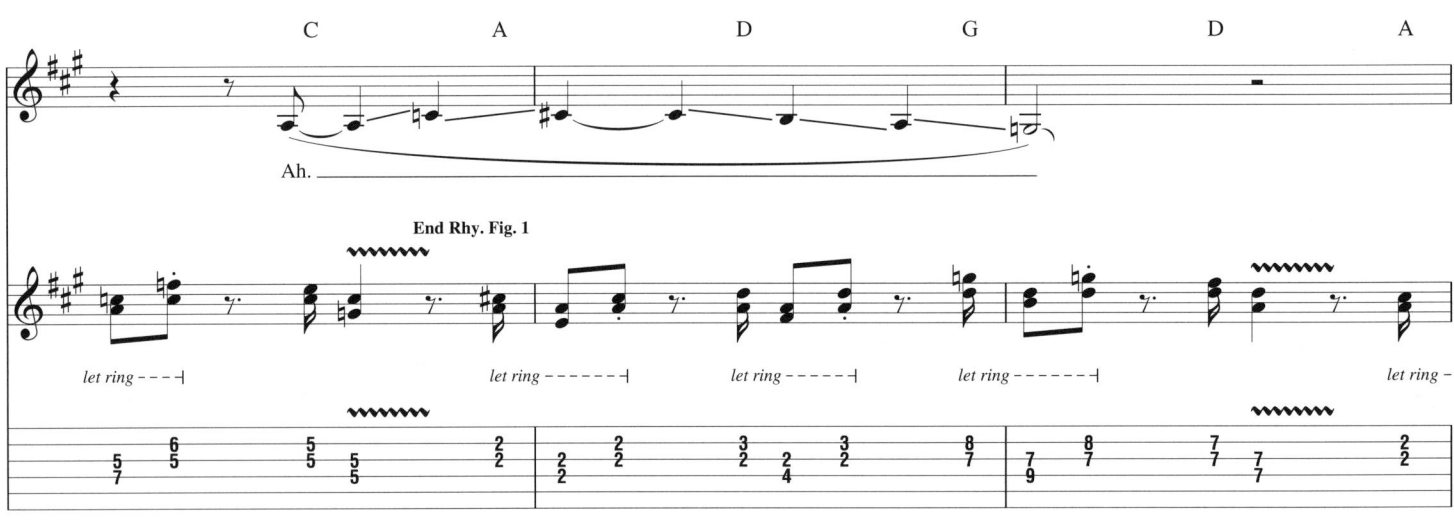

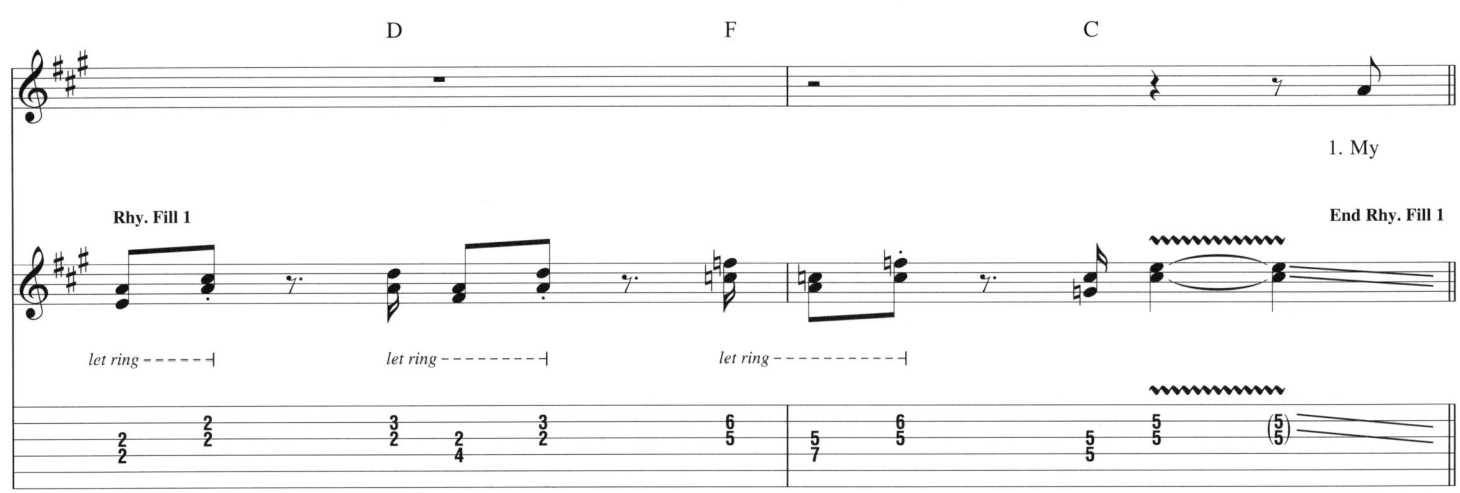

Copyright © 1976 HORI PRODUCTIONS AMERICA, INC. and CAFE AMERICANA
Copyright Renewed
All Rights for HORI PRODUCTIONS AMERICA, INC. Controlled and Administered by UNIVERSAL - POLYGRAM INTERNATIONAL PUBLISHING, INC.
All Rights for CAFE AMERICANA in the U.S. Administered by INTERSONG U.S.A., INC.
All Rights outside the U.S. excluding Japan Controlled and Administered by UNIVERSAL - POLYGRAM INTERNATIONAL PUBLISHING, INC.
All Rights Reserved   Used by Permission

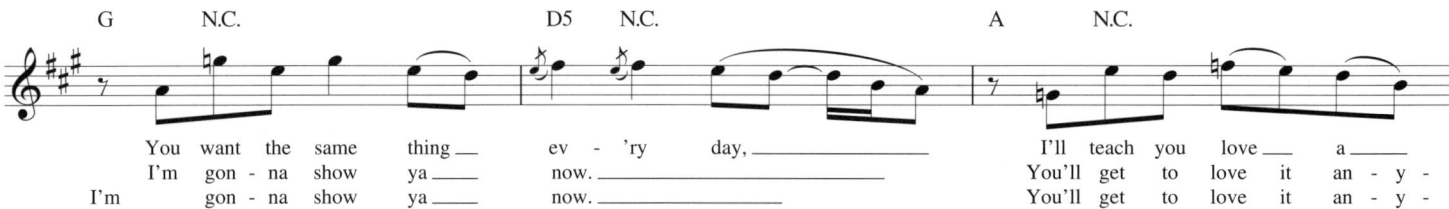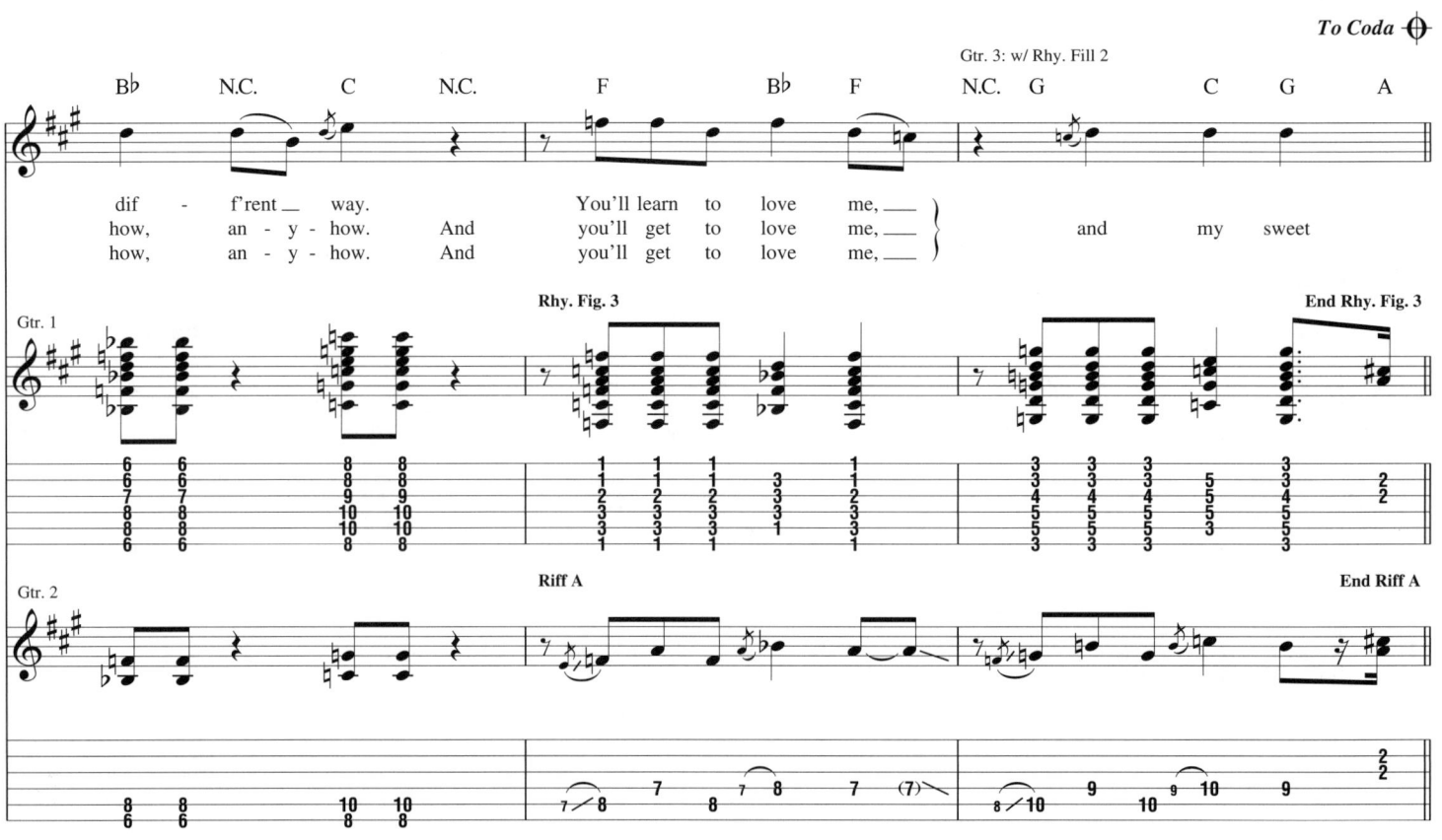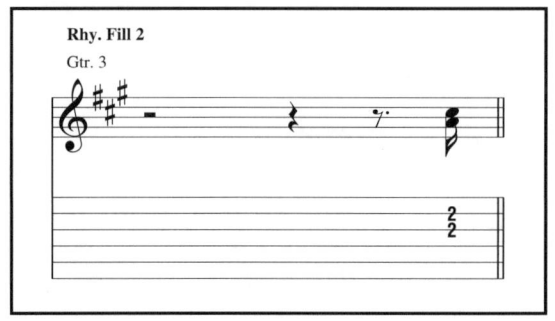

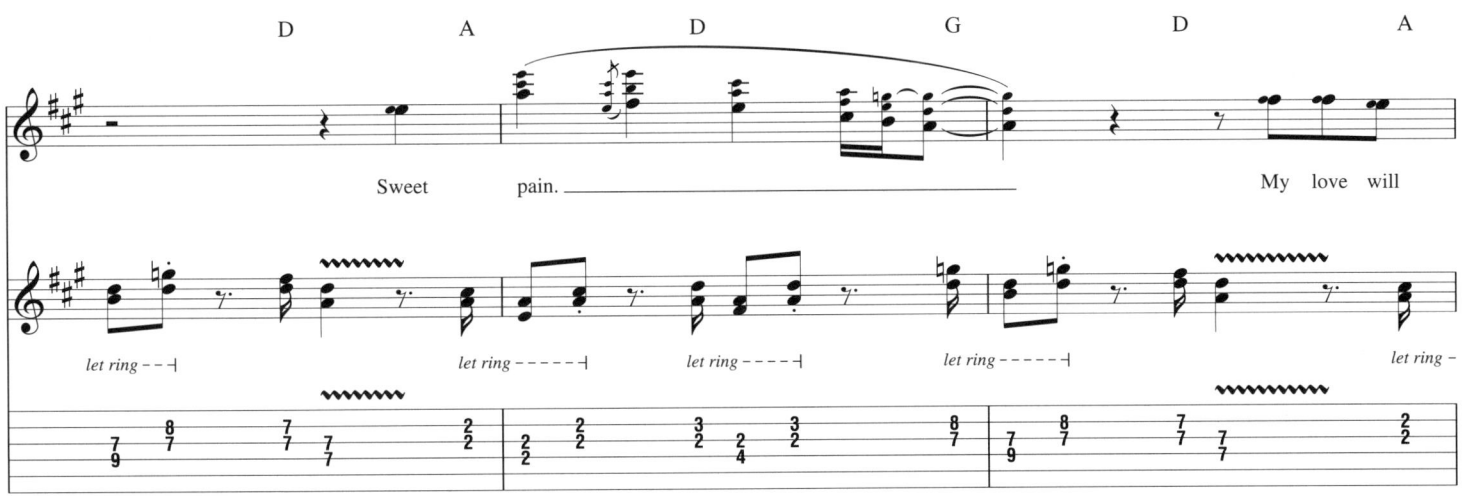
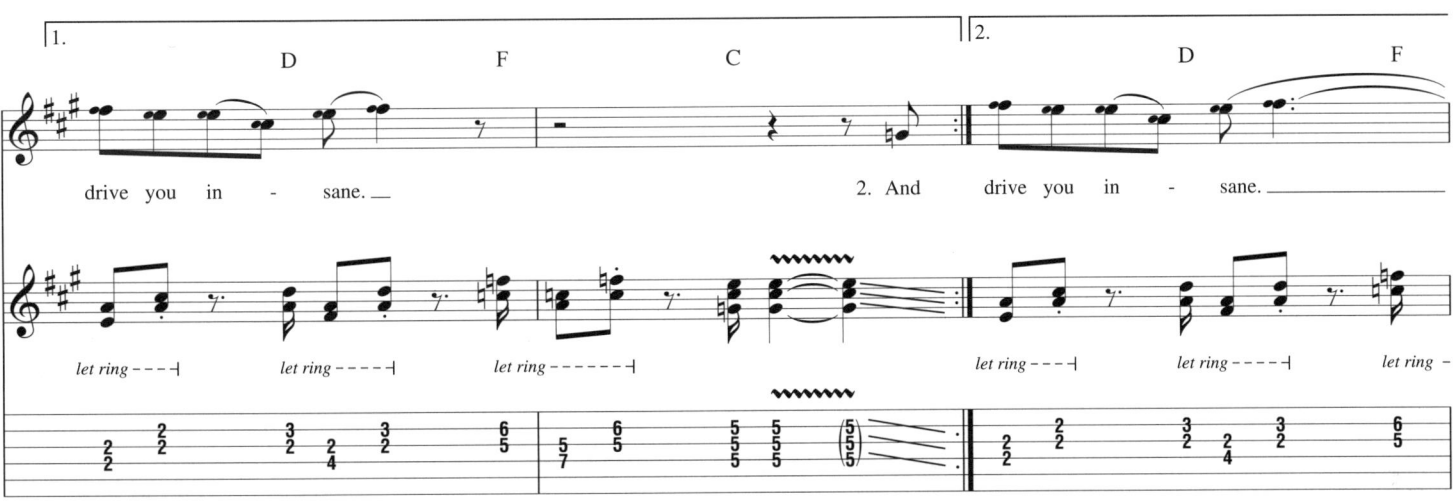
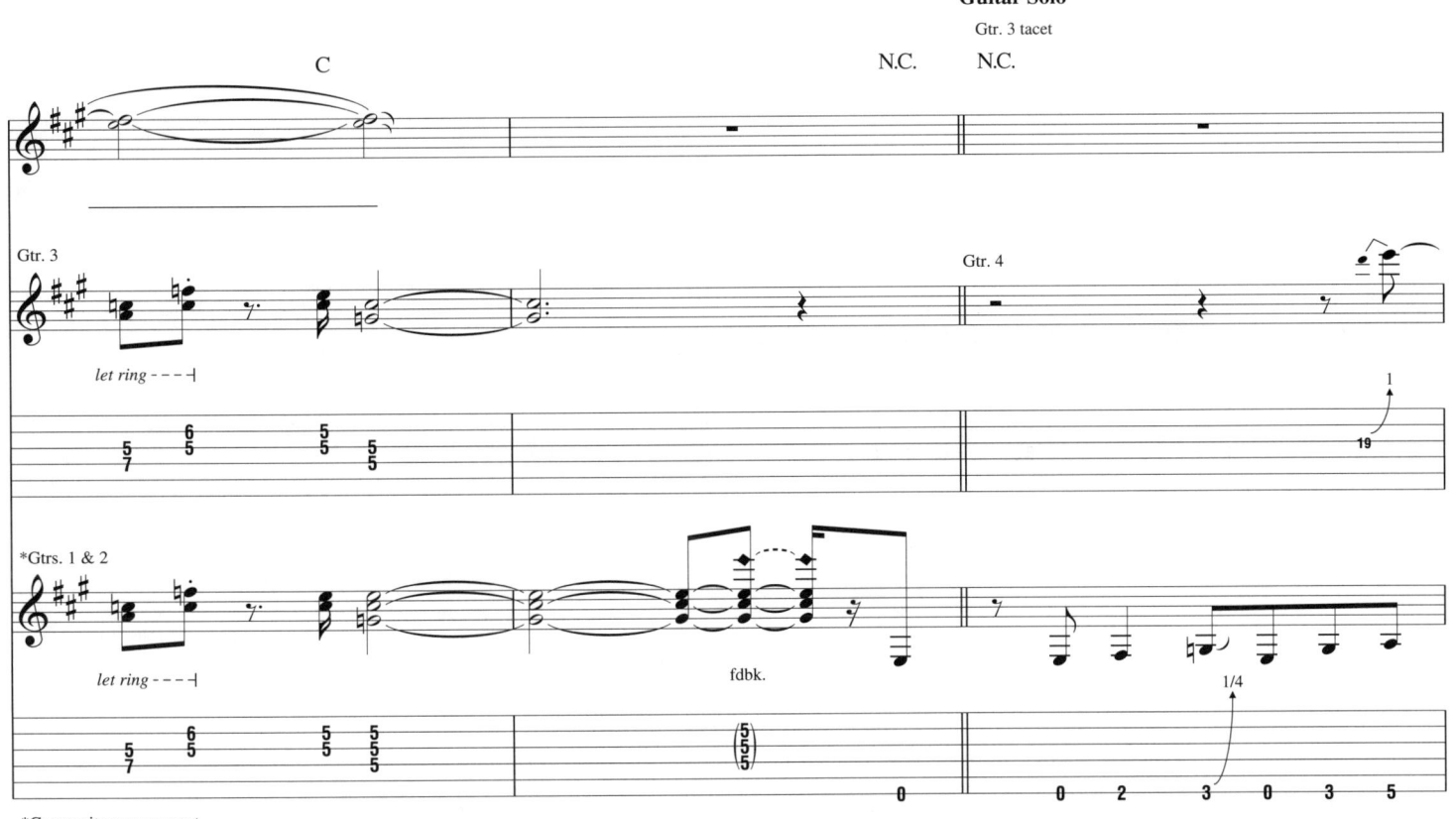

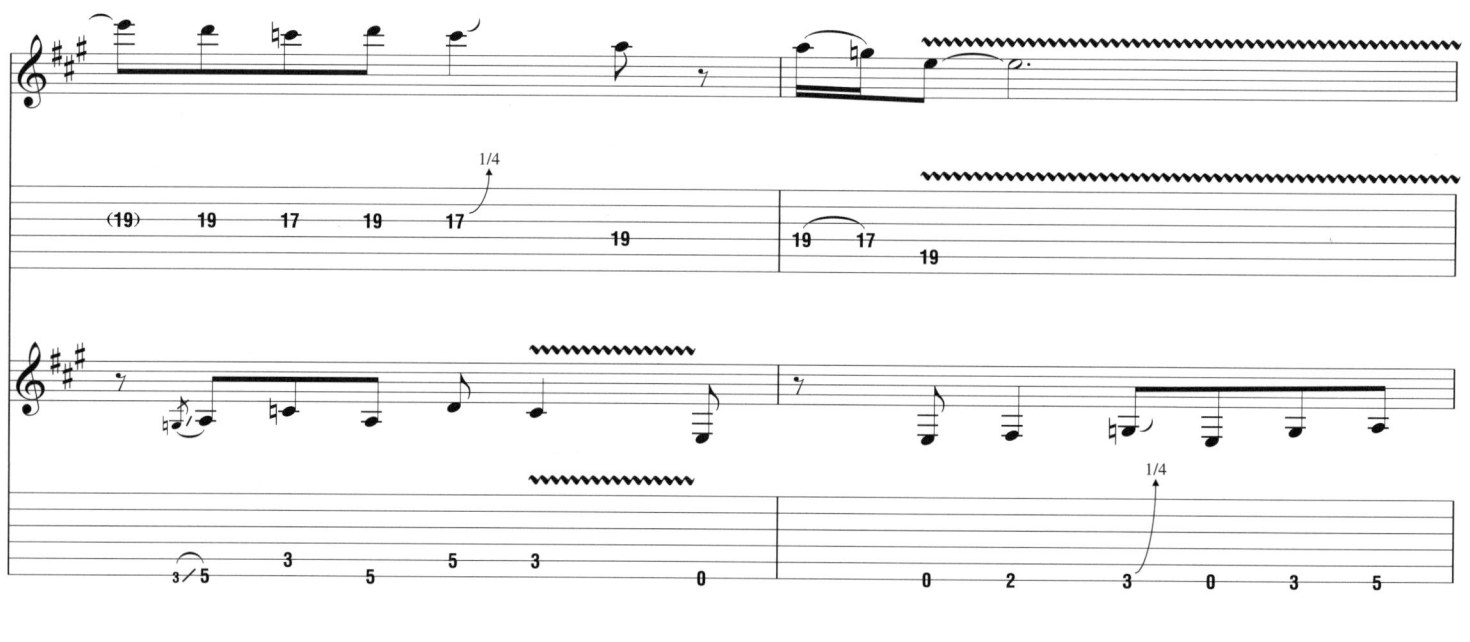
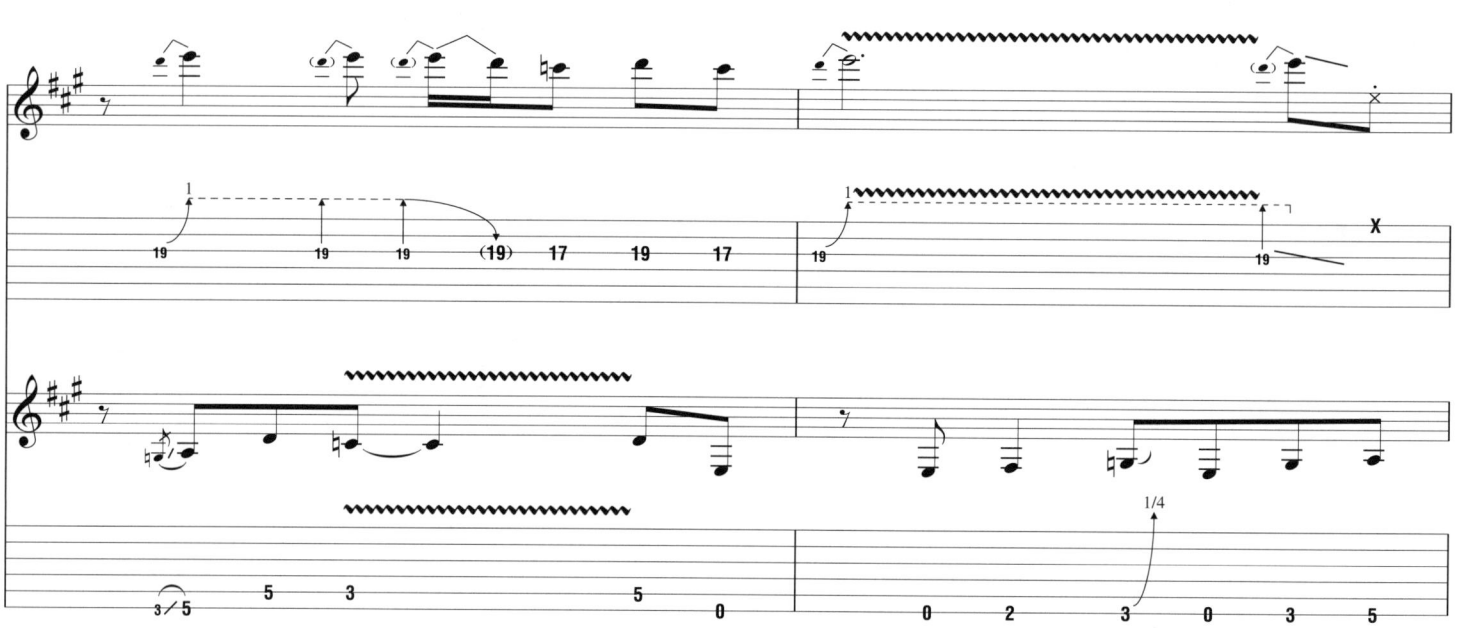
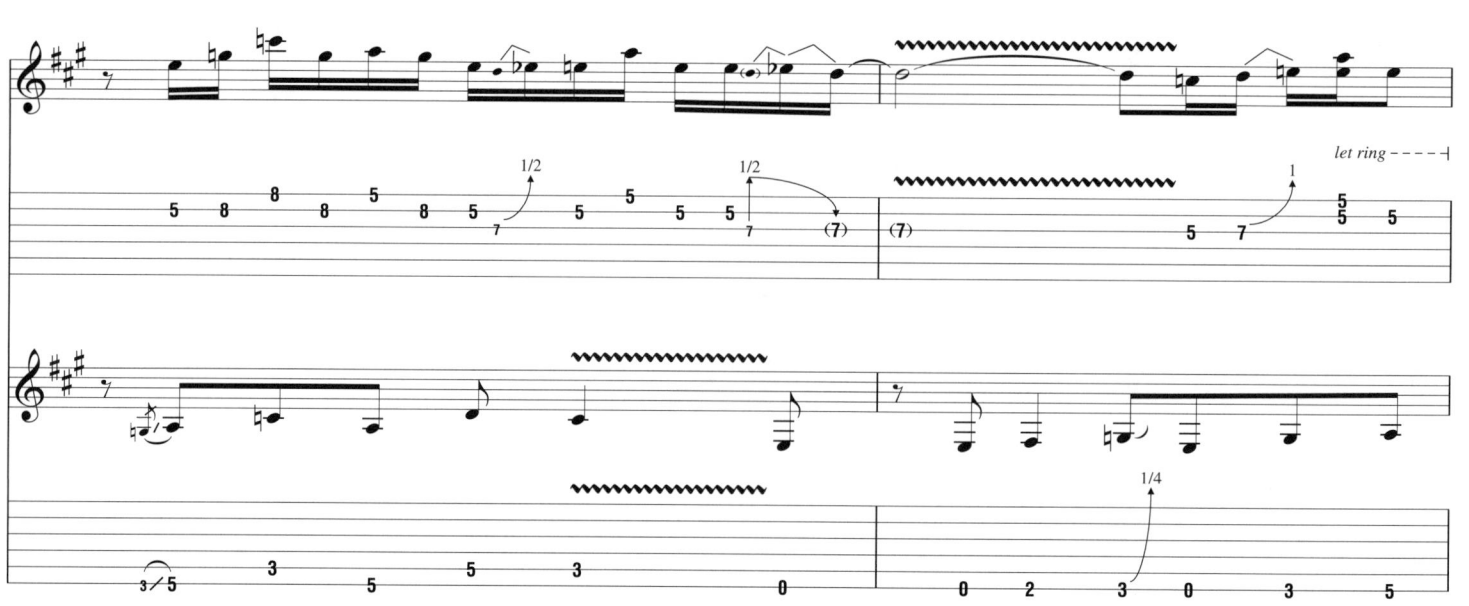

42

Bridge
Gtr. 3: w/ Rhy. Fill 2
N.C. F Bb F N.C. G C G A
Ah. You'll get to love me any - y way I say.
Gtr. 4
fdbk.
grad. release
let ring
Gtr. 1
Gtr. 2

Gtr. 1: w/ Rhy. Fig. 3
Gtr. 2: w/ Riff A
Gtr. 3 tacet
D G D N.C. F Bb F
Ah. You'll get to love me
Gtr. 4
P.H.
Pitch: A B A
Gtrs. 1, 2 & 3
let ring
let ring
let ring

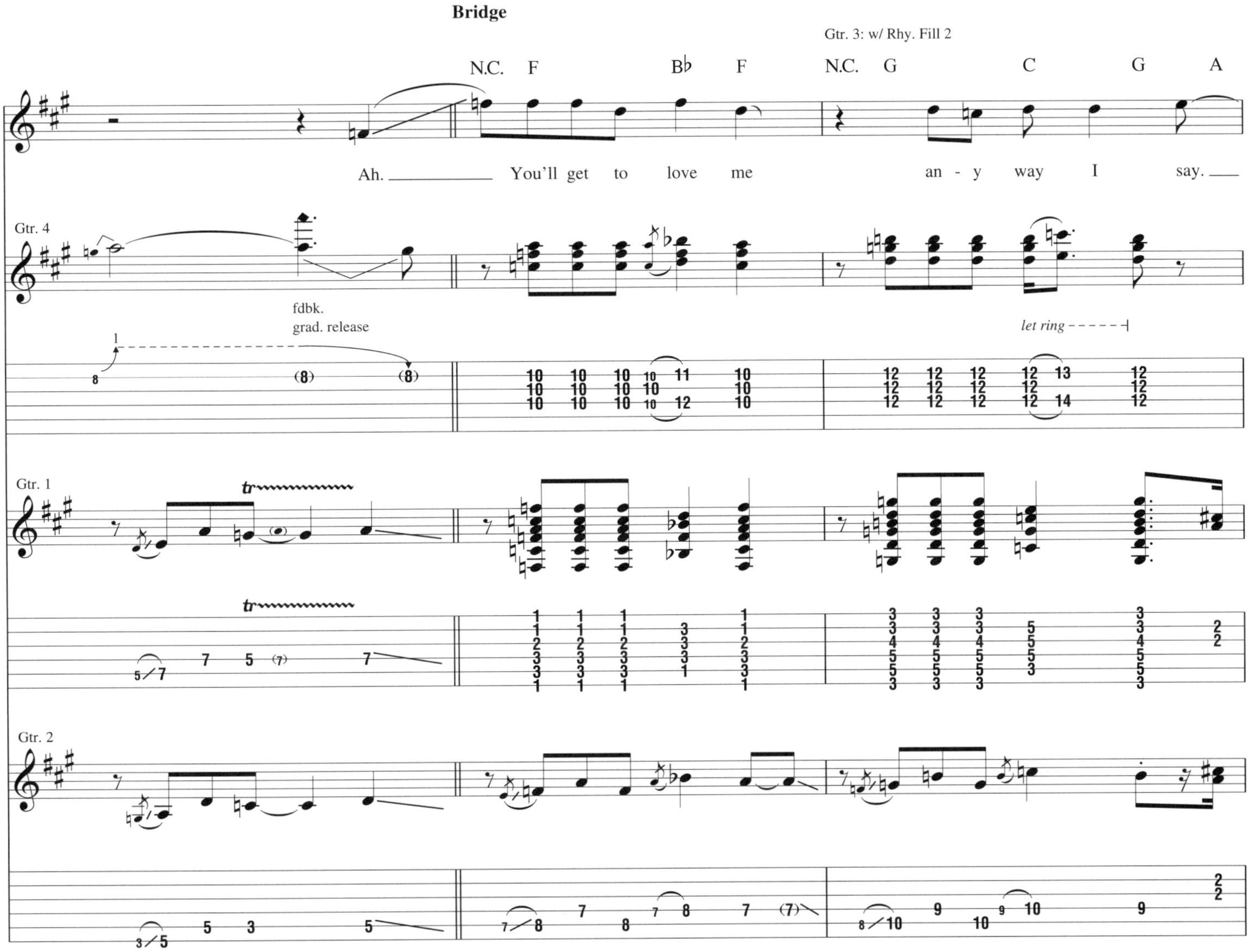

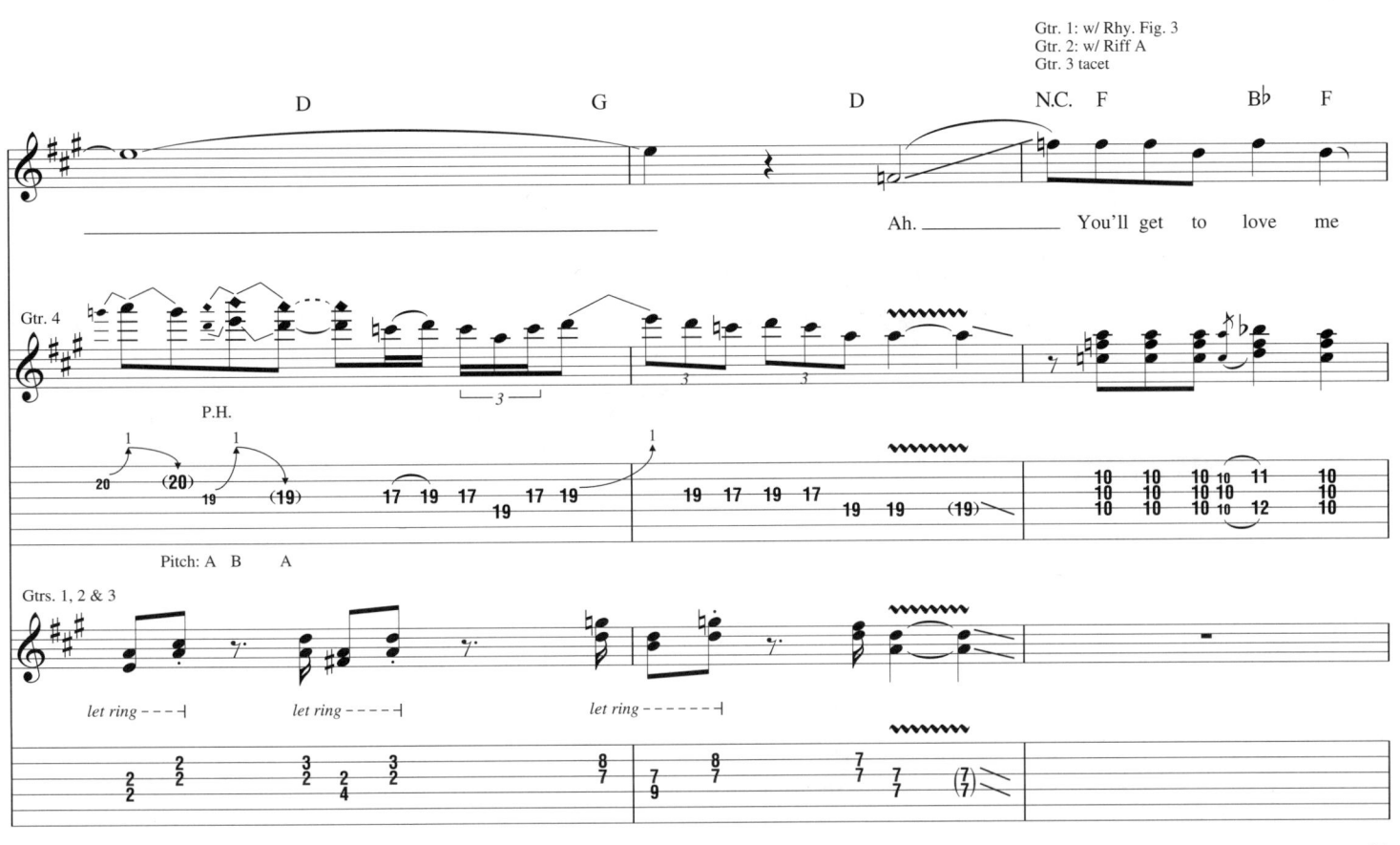

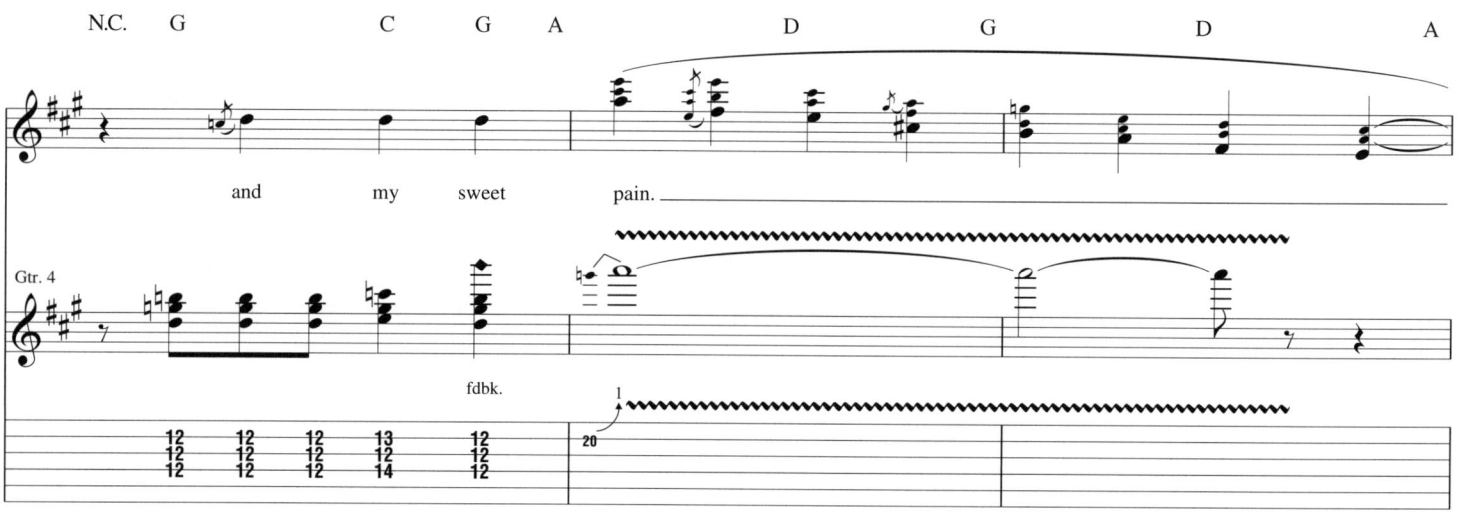
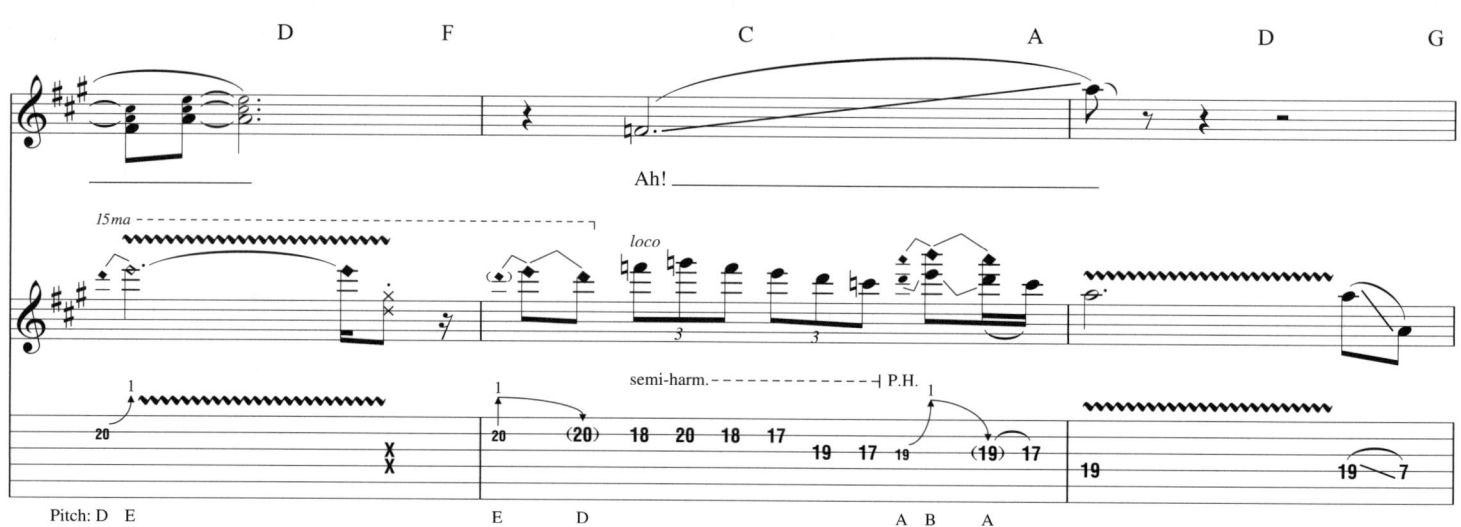
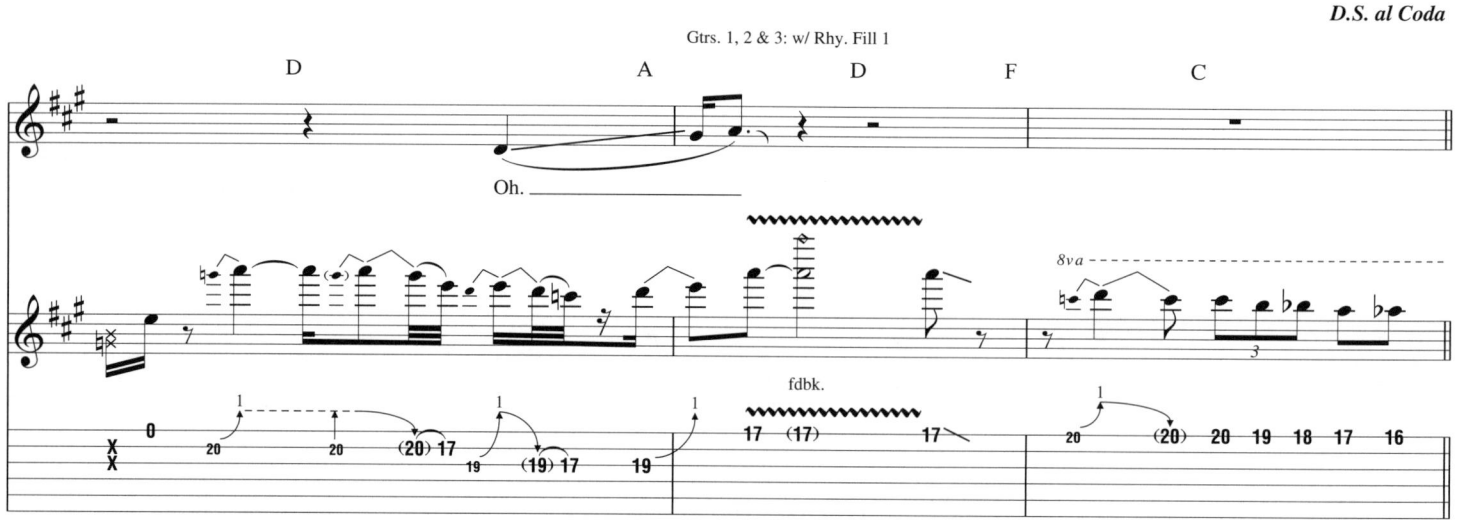
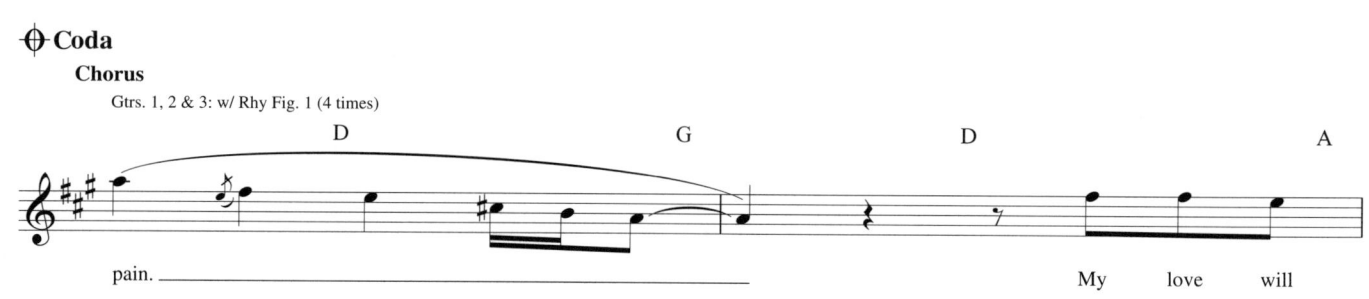

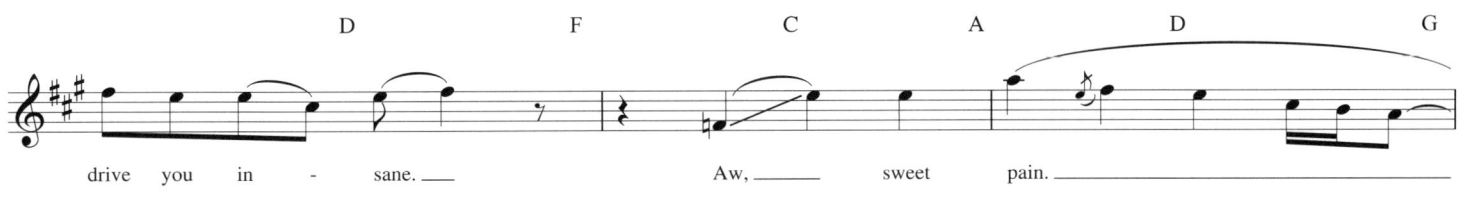
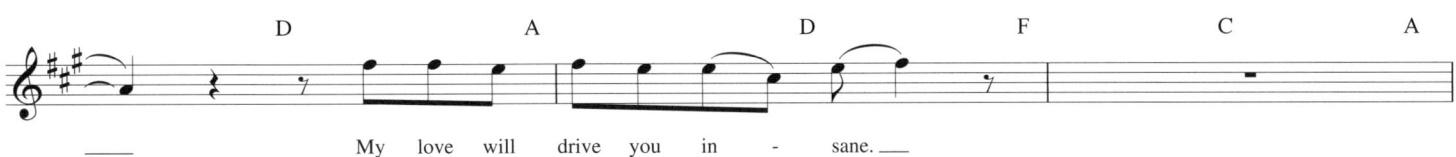
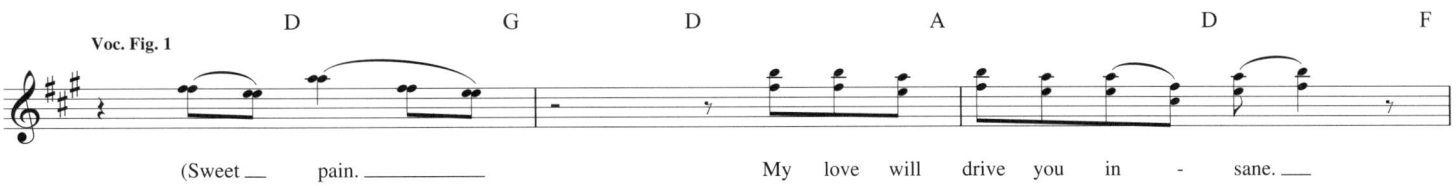
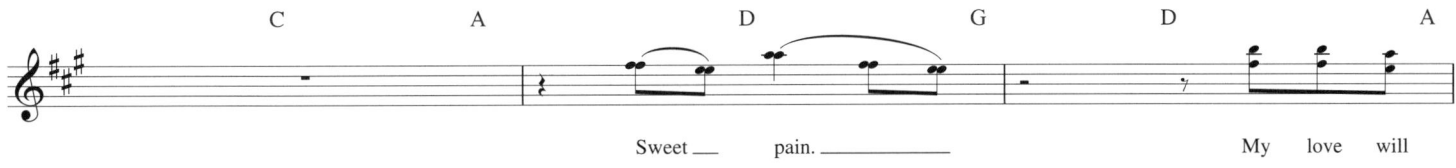

Outro-Chorus
Bkgd. Voc.: w/ Voc. Fig. 1 (till fade)
Gtrs. 1, 2 & 3: w/ Rhy. Fig. 1 (till fade)

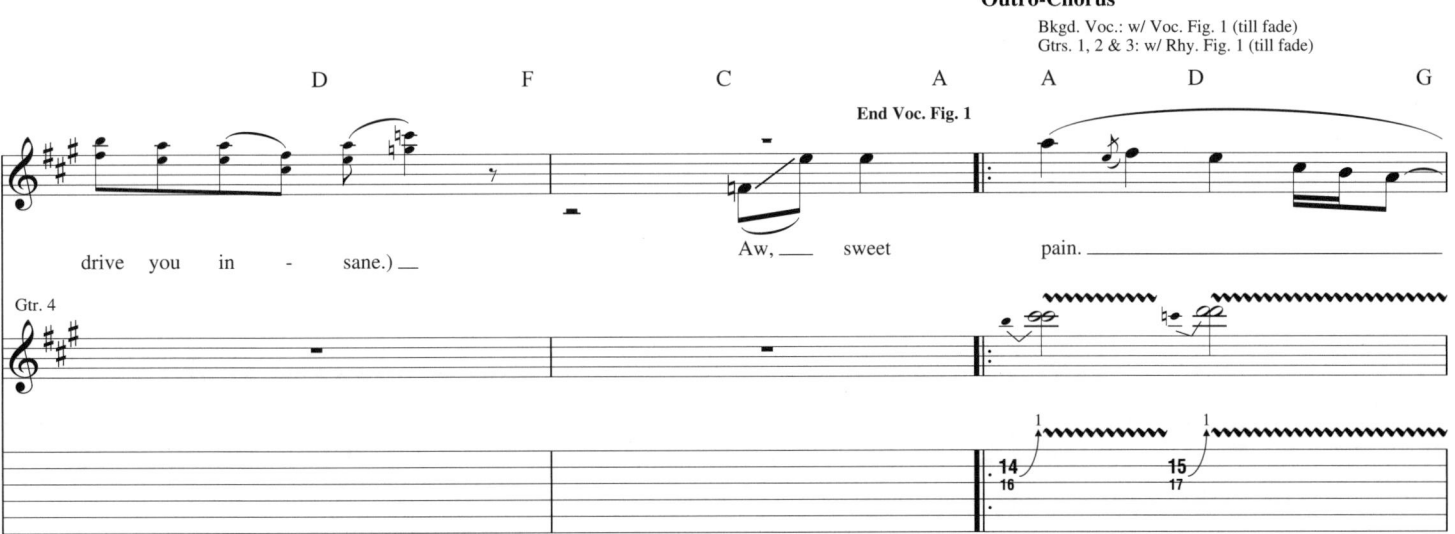

Play 4 times and fade

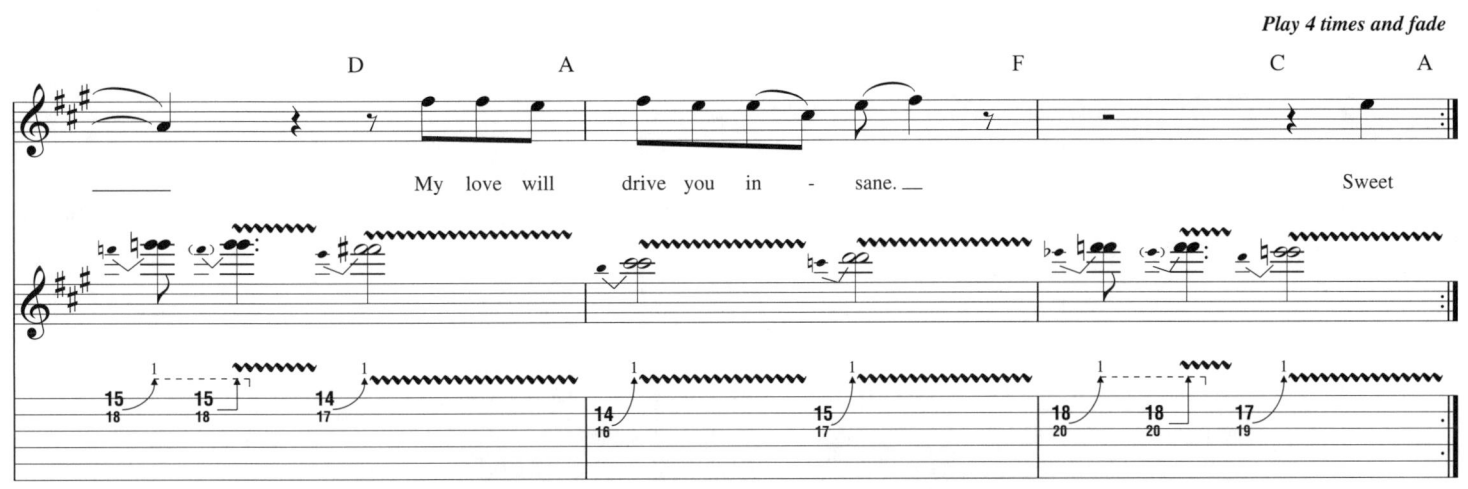

Shout It Out Loud

Words and Music by Paul Stanley, Gene Simmons and Bob Ezrin

Tune down 1/2 step:
(low to high) Eb-Ab-Db-Gb-Bb-Eb

Intro
Moderately fast Rock ♩ = 152

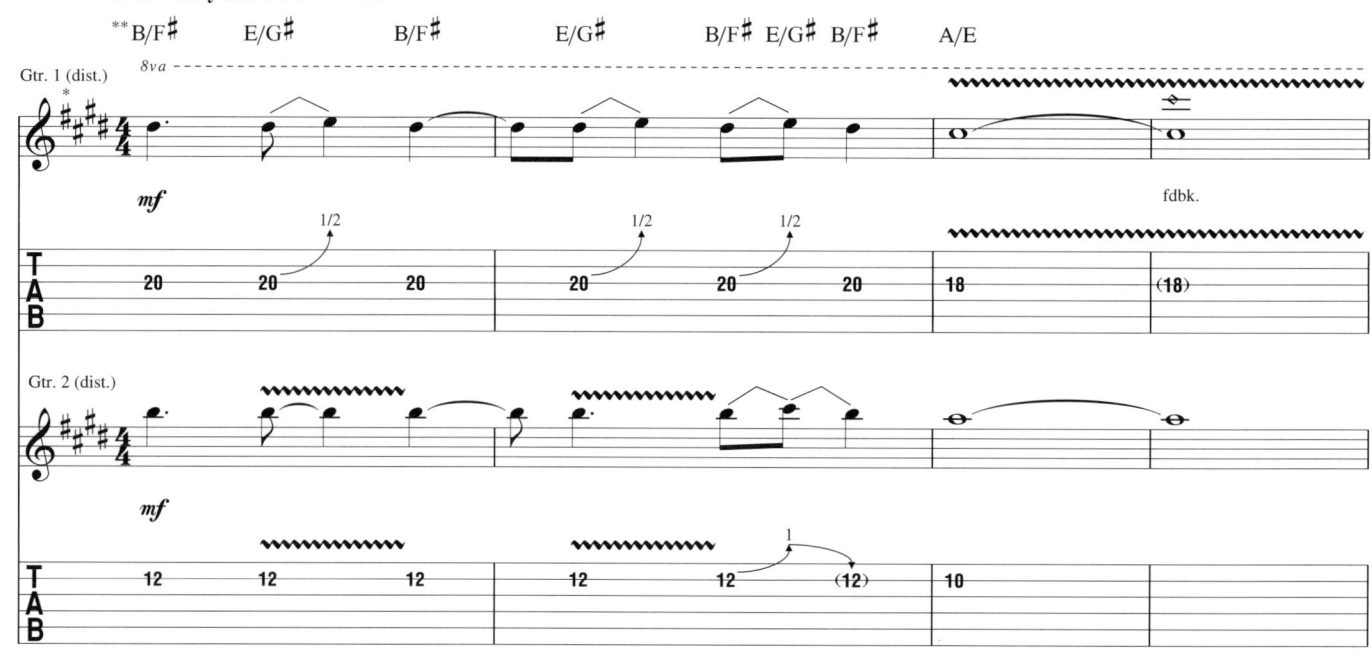

*Key signature denotes B Mixolydian.
**Chord symbols reflect overall harmony.

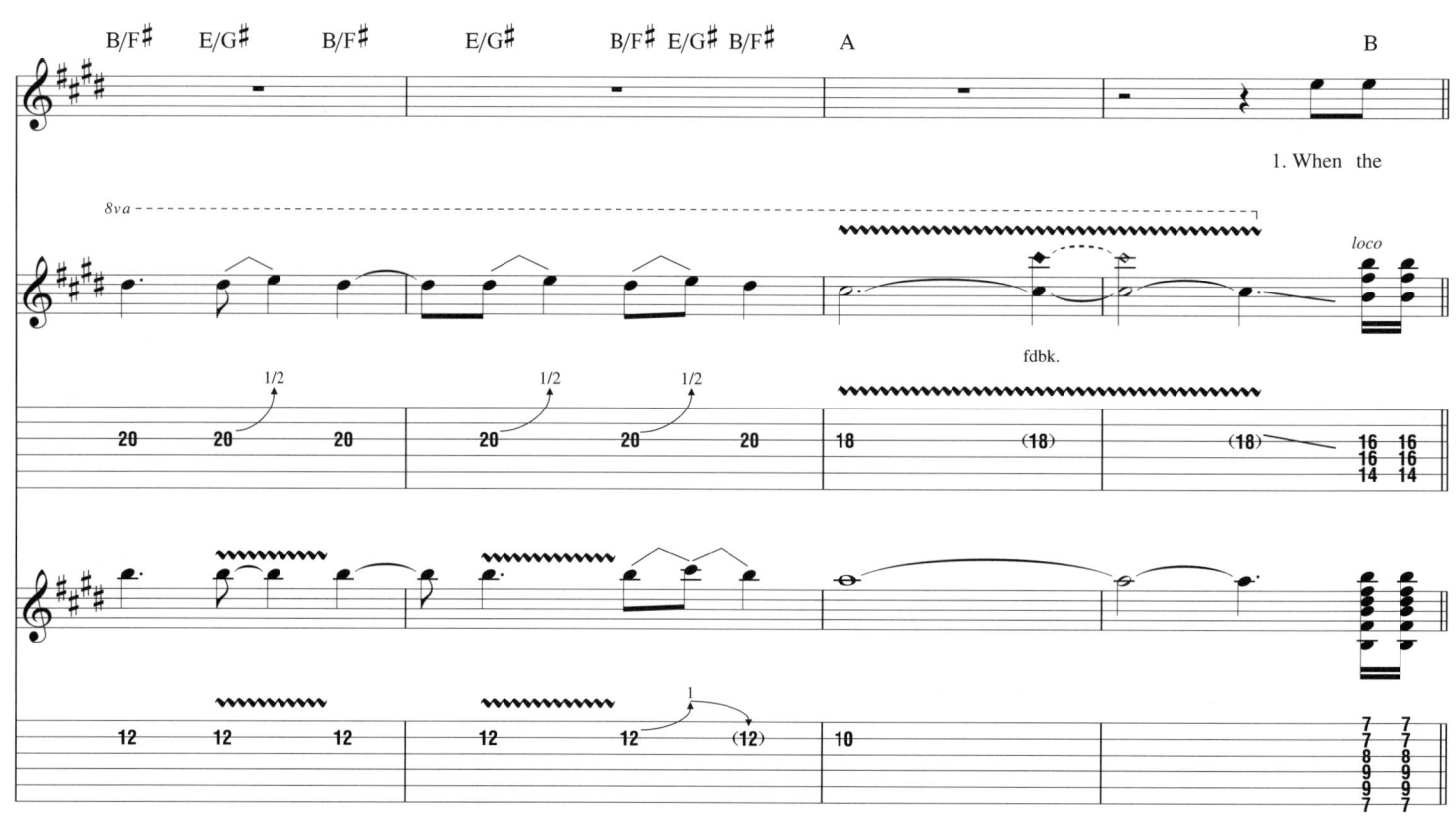

Copyright © 1976 HORI PRODUCTIONS AMERICA, INC., ALL BY MYSELF MUSIC and CAFE AMERICANA
Copyright Renewed
All Rights for HORI PRODUCTIONS AMERICA, INC. and ALL BY MYSELF MUSIC Controlled and Administered by
UNIVERSAL - POLYGRAM INTERNATIONAL PUBLISHING, INC.
All Rights for CAFE AMERICANA in the U.S. Administered by INTERSONG U.S.A., INC.
All Rights outside the U.S. excluding Japan Controlled and Administered by UNIVERSAL - POLYGRAM INTERNATIONAL PUBLISHING, INC.
All Rights Reserved   Used by Permission

Verse

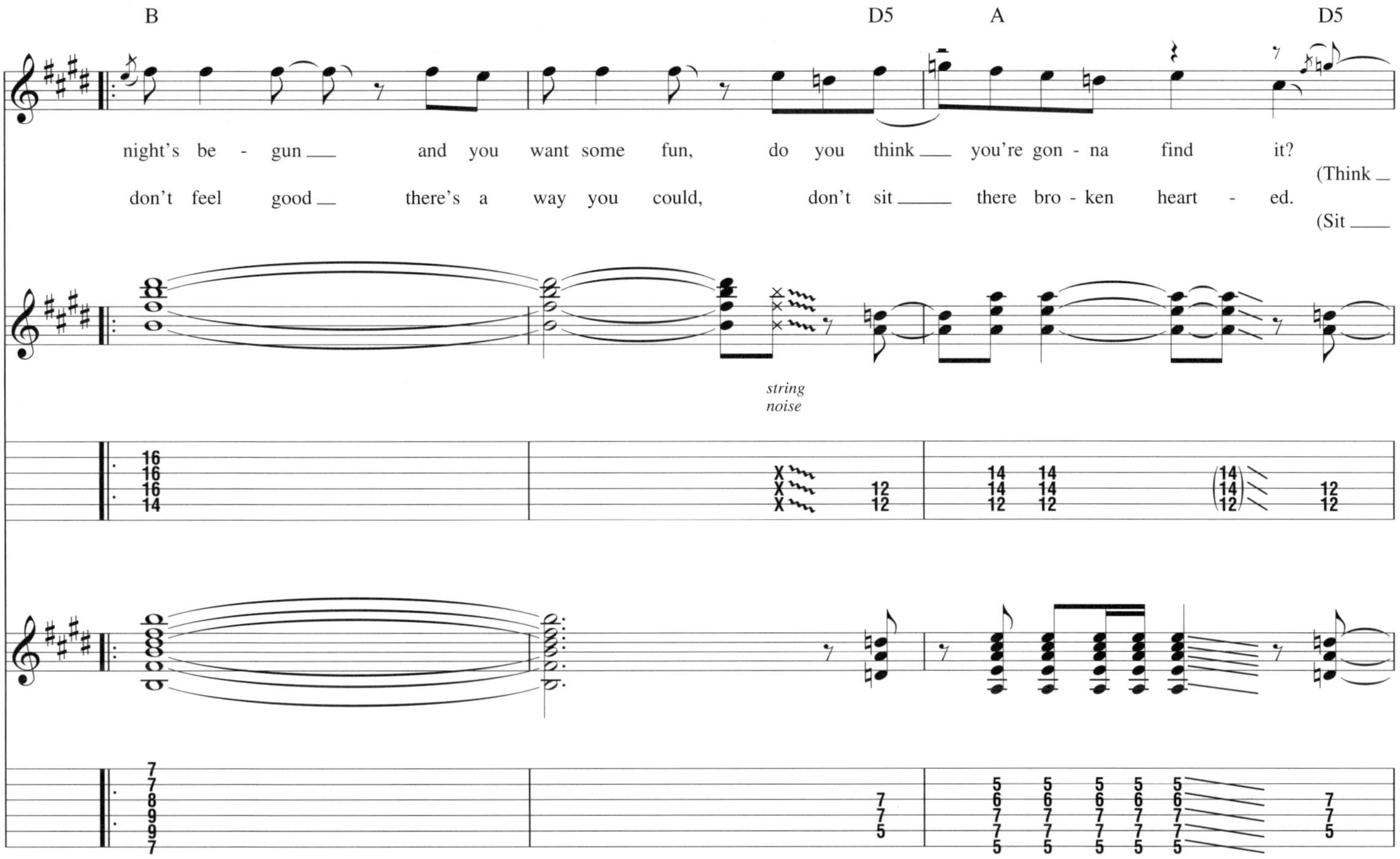

night's be-gun ___ and you want some fun, do you think ___ you're gon-na find it? (Think ___
don't feel good ___ there's a way you could, don't sit ___ there bro-ken heart-ed. (Sit ___

string noise

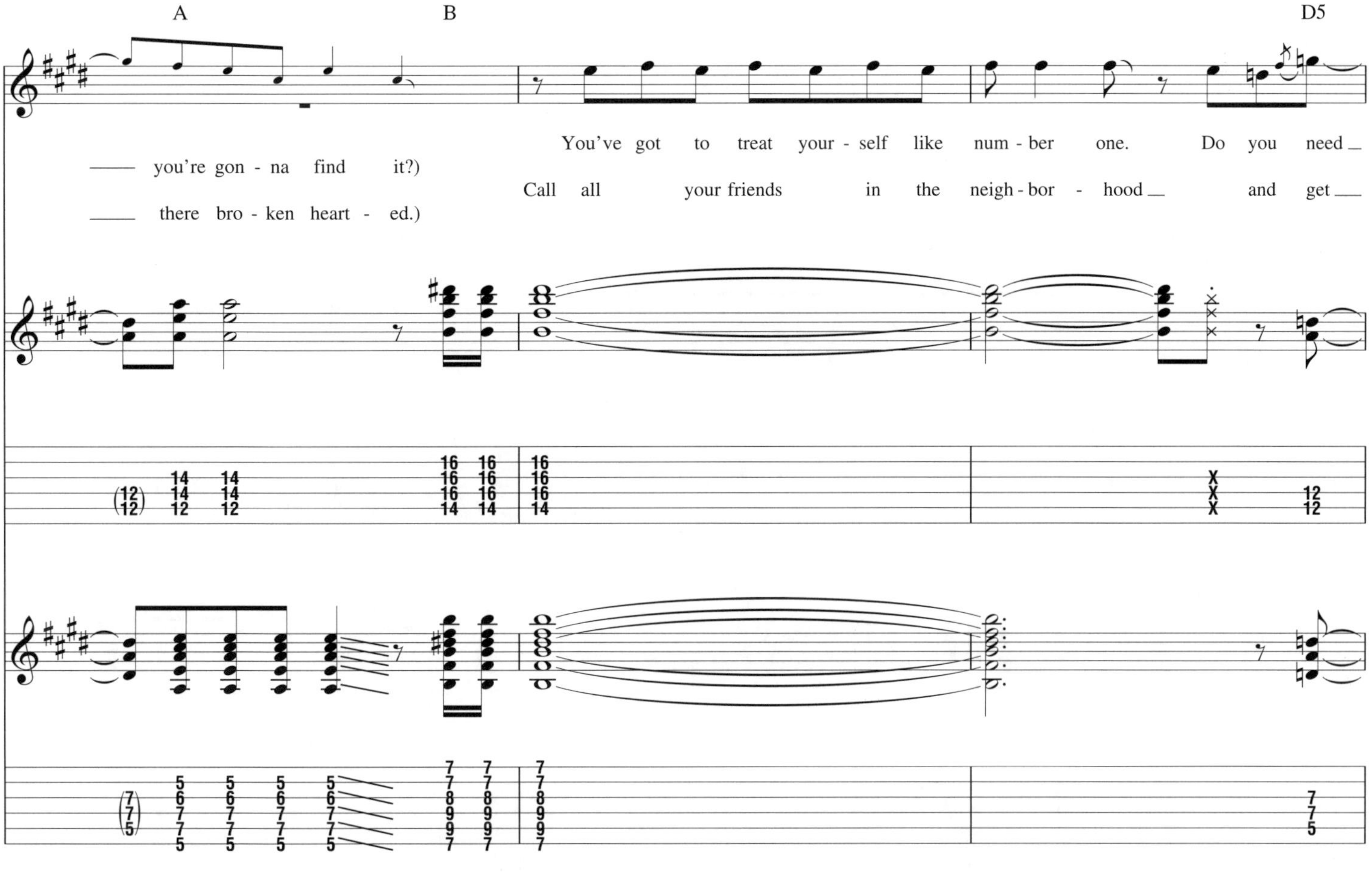

___ you're gon-na find it?) You've got to treat your-self like num-ber one. Do you need ___
___ there bro-ken heart - ed.) Call all your friends in the neigh-bor-hood ___ and get ___

	A		D5	A	

_____ to be re - mind - ed?
_____ the par - ty start - ed. (Need _____ to be re - mind - ed.)
(Get _____ the par - ty start - ed.)

steady gliss.

Pre-Chorus

D	G/D	D	D6	D	G/D	D	D6	A5	D/A	A	E5

It does - n't mat - ter what you do or say. Just for - get _____ the things that you've been _____ told. _____
Don't let 'em tell you that there's too much noise. They're too old _____ to real - ly un - der - stand. _____

Rhy. Fig. 1

Rhy. Fig. 1A

D/E E D G/D D G/D D G/D D A5
We can't do it an - y oth - er way. Ev - 'ry - bod -
You'll still get row - dy with the girls and boys, cause it's time
D/A A B
- y's got to rock and roll. Whoa.
for you to take a stand. Yeah, and...
End Rhy. Fig. 1
End Rhy. Fig. 1A
fdbk.

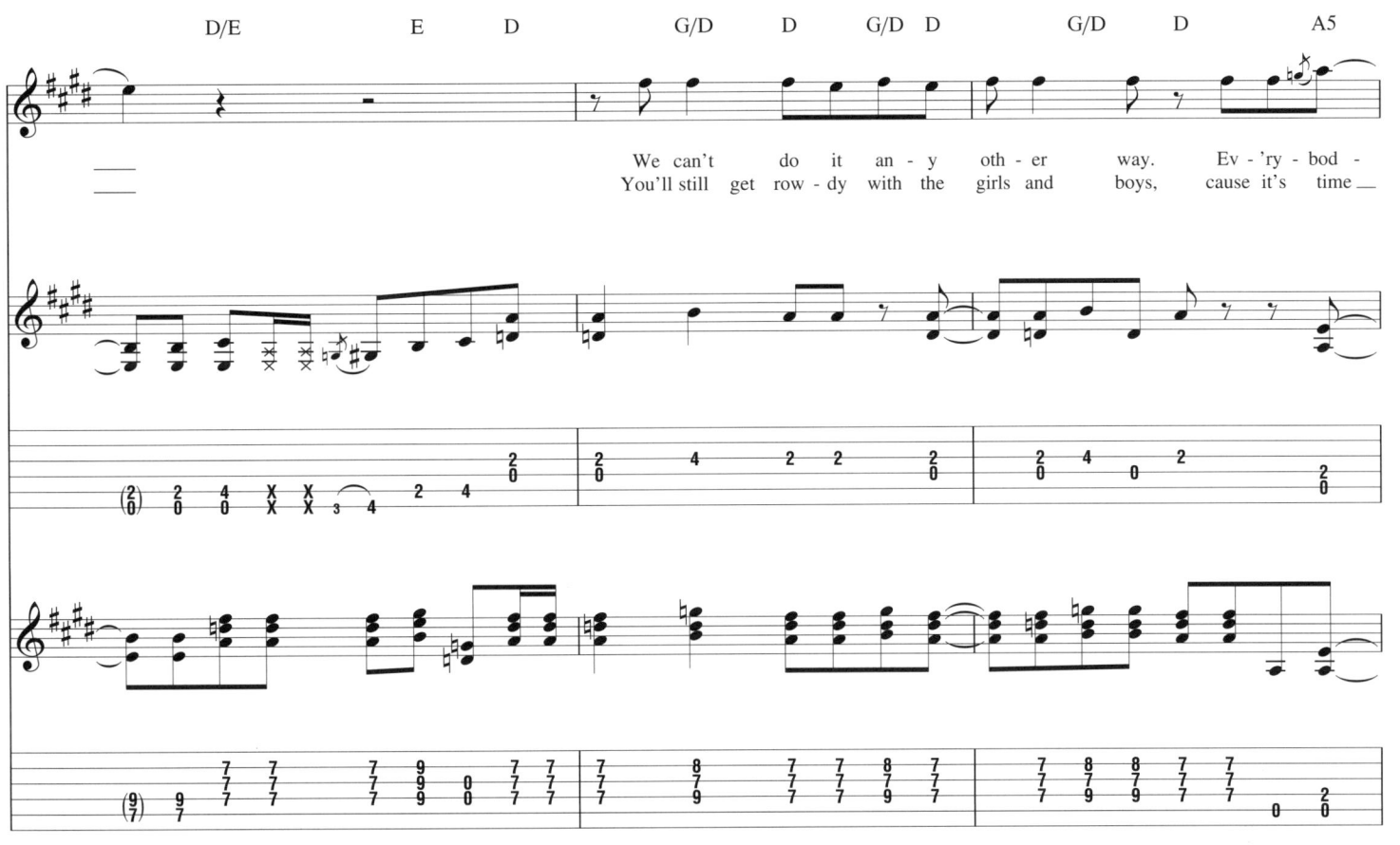

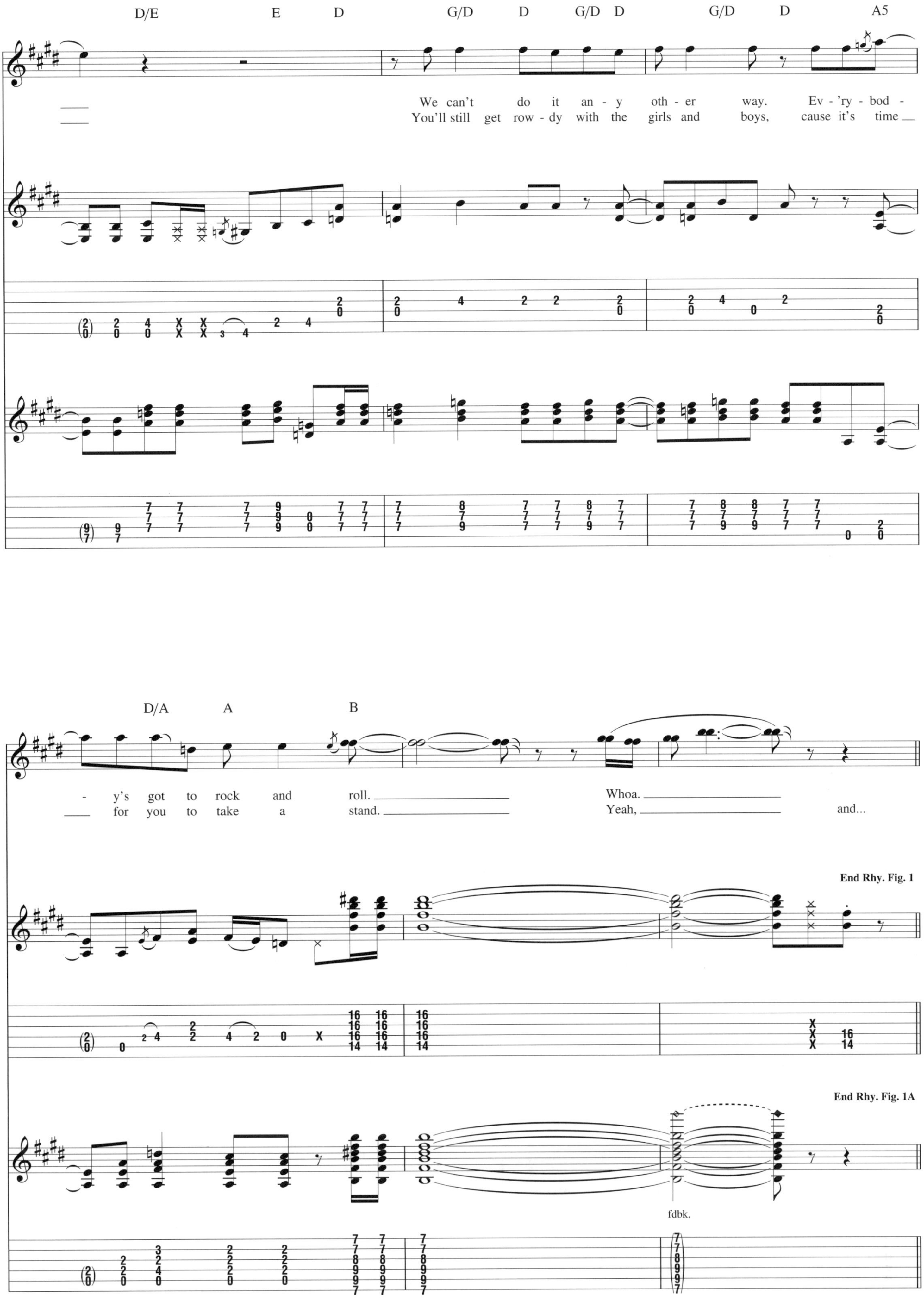

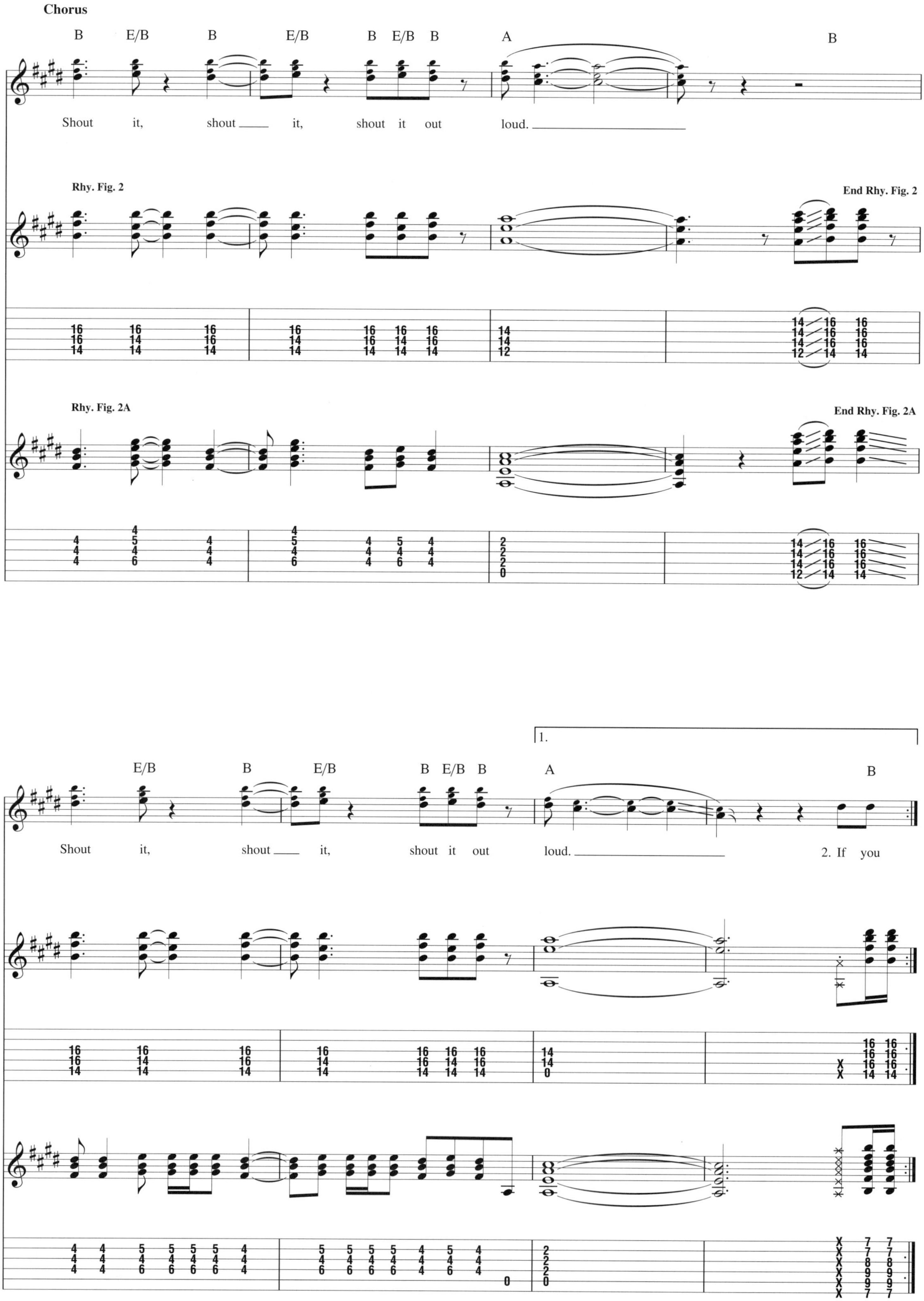
Chorus
B E/B B E/B B E/B B A B
Shout it, shout it, shout it out loud.
Rhy. Fig. 2
End Rhy. Fig. 2
Rhy. Fig. 2A
End Rhy. Fig. 2A
1.
E/B B E/B B E/B B A B
Shout it, shout it, shout it out loud.
2. If you

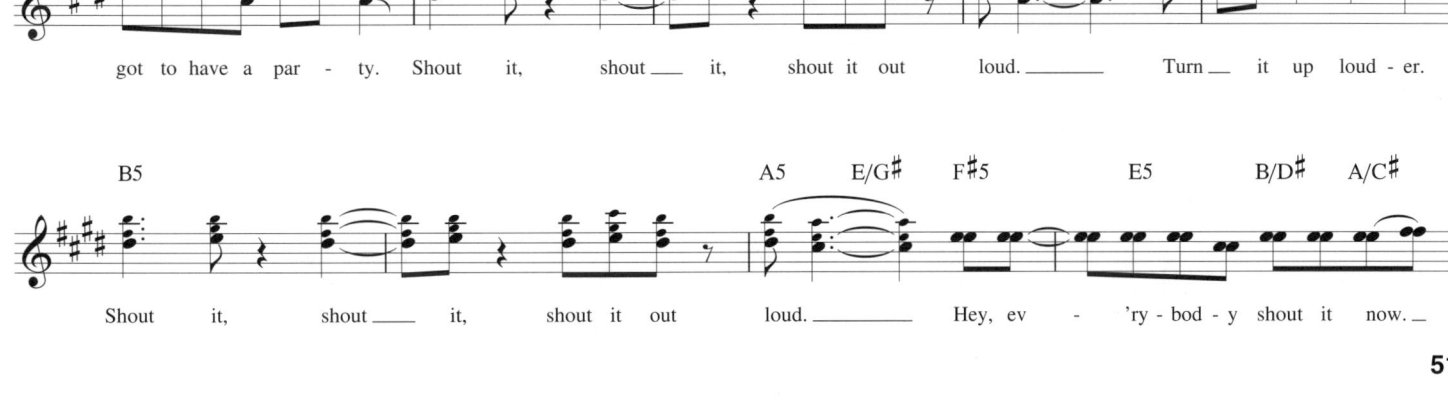

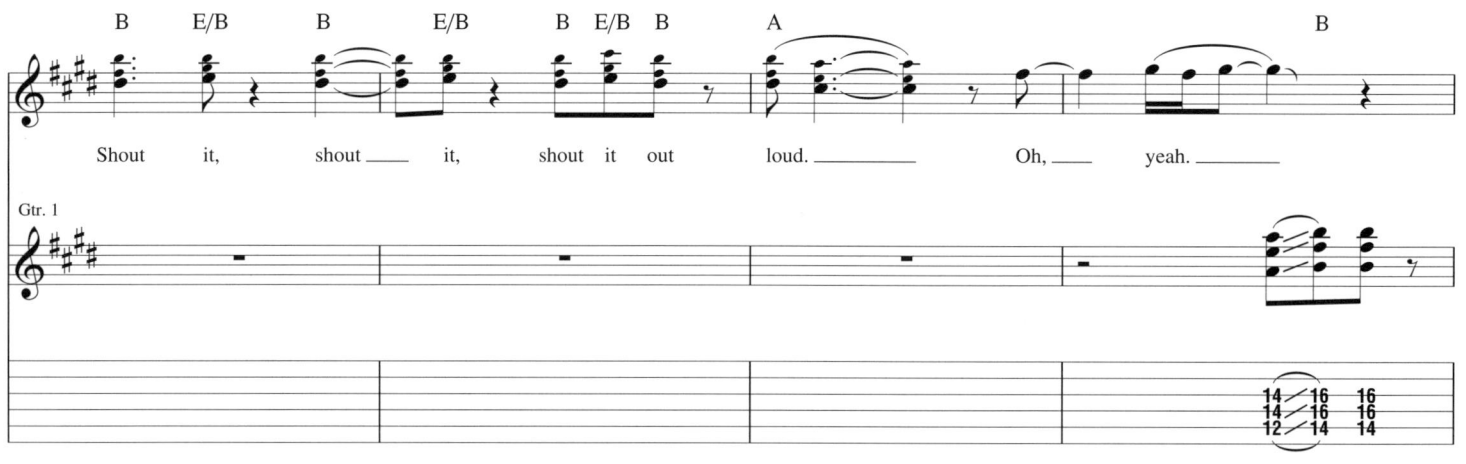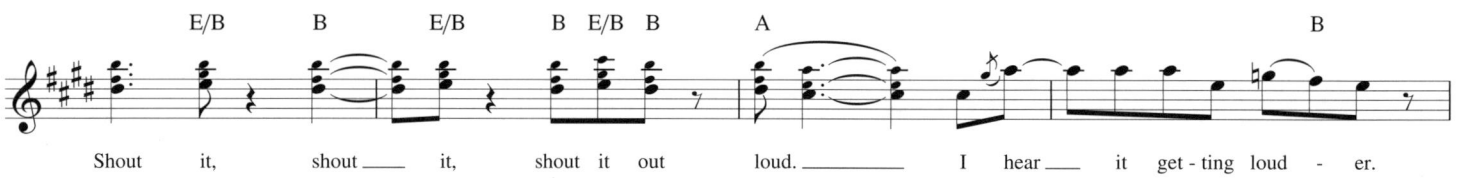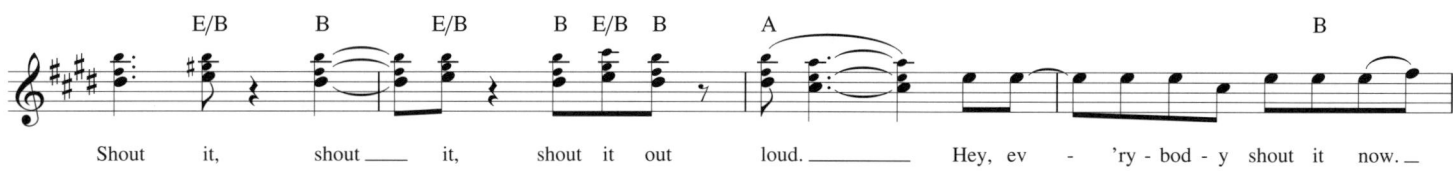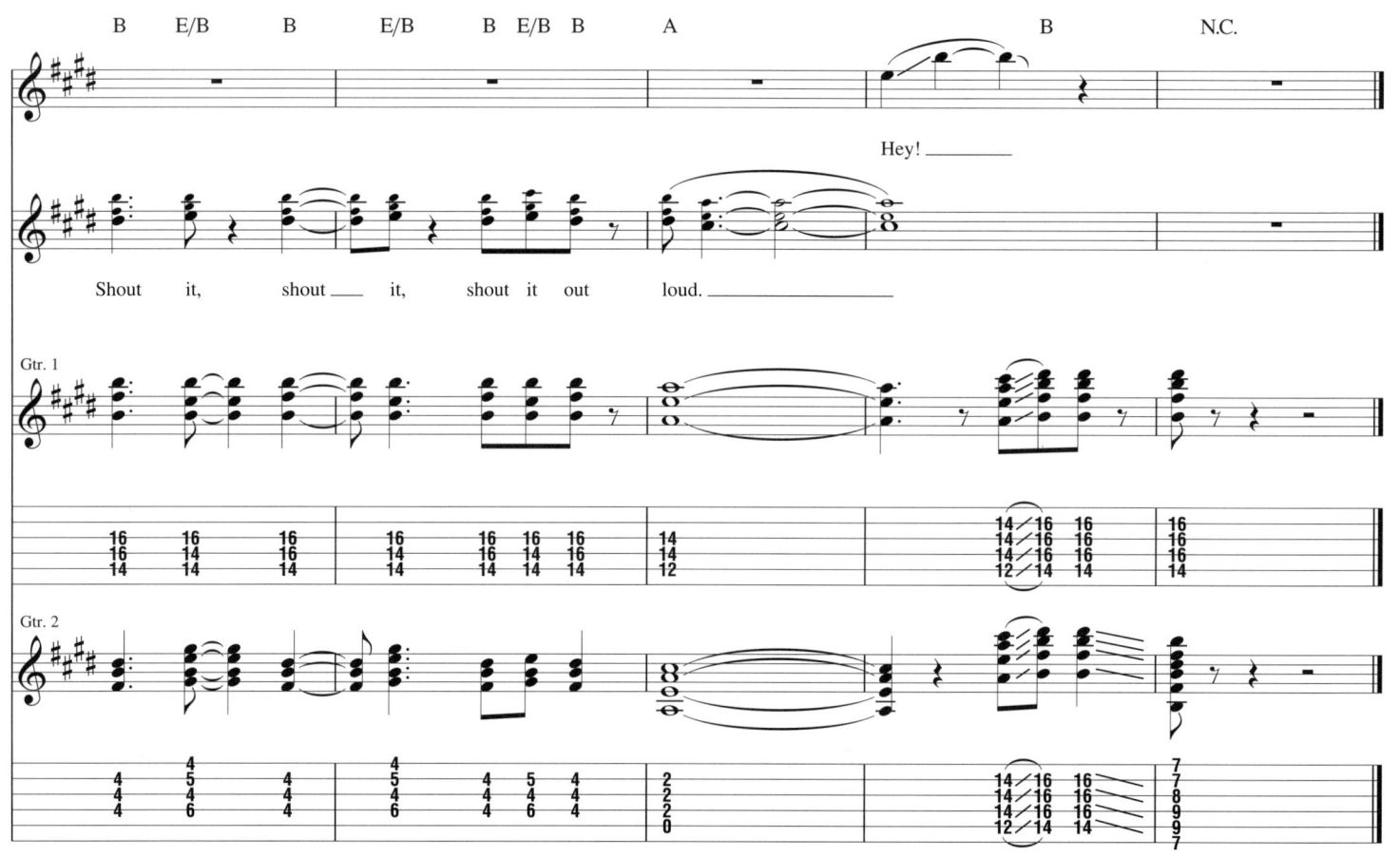

Beth

Words and Music by Bob Ezrin, Stanley Penridge and Peter Criss

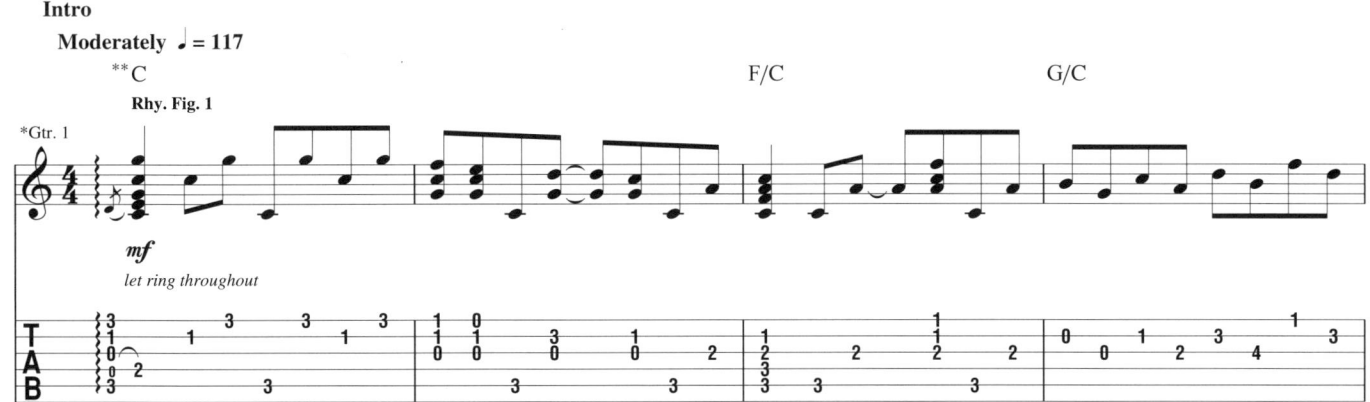

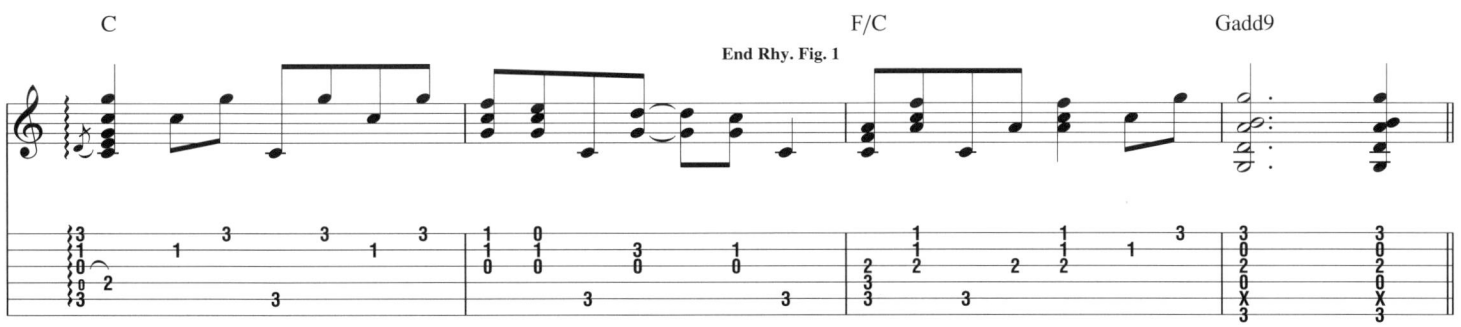

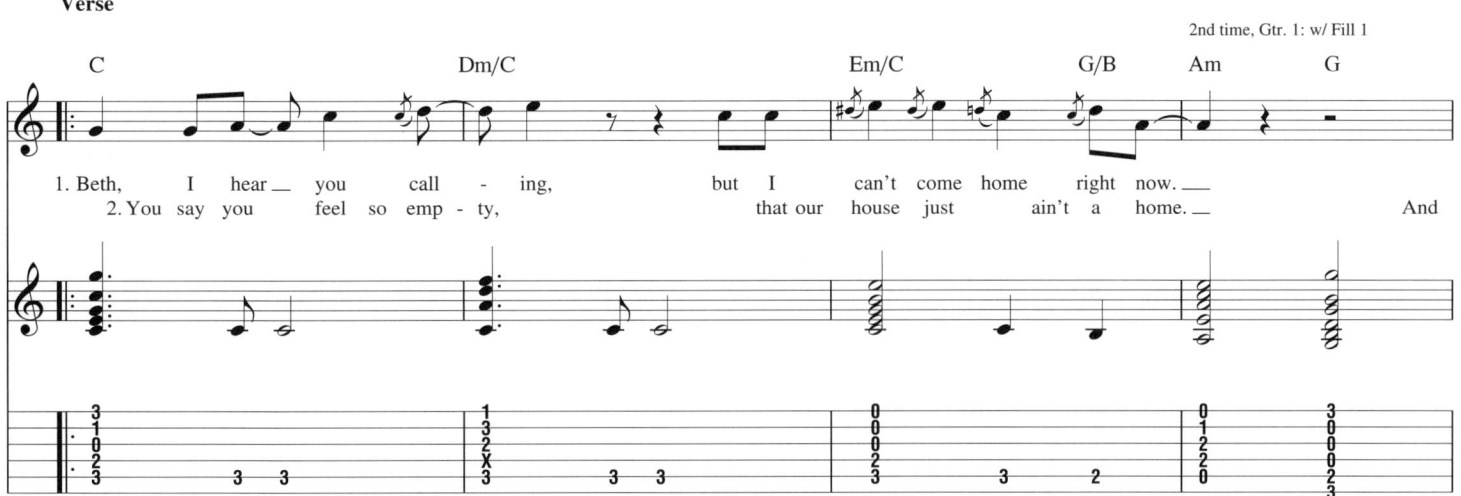

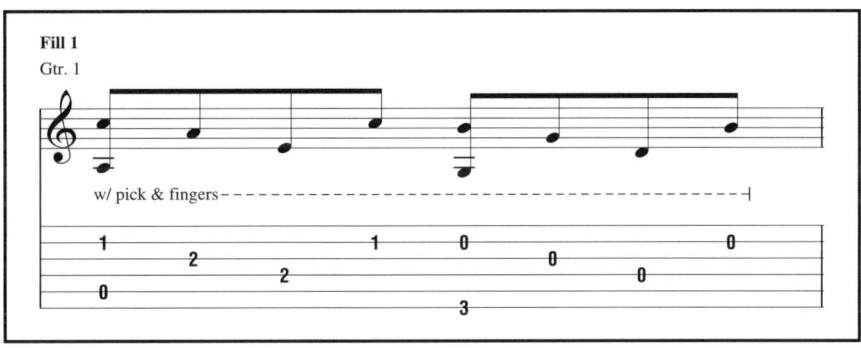

Copyright © 1976 ROCK STEADY MUSIC, ALL BY MYSELF PUBLISHING CO., CAFE AMERICANA and PETER CRISS PUBLISHING
Copyright Renewed
All Rights for ROCK STEADY MUSIC Controlled and Administered by UNIVERSAL - POLYGRAM INTERNATIONAL PUBLISHING, INC.
All Rights for ALL BY MYSELF PUBLISHING CO. Controlled and Administered by IRVING MUSIC, INC.
All Rights for CAFE AMERICANA Controlled and Administered by CHAPPELL & CO.
All Rights Reserved   Used by Permission

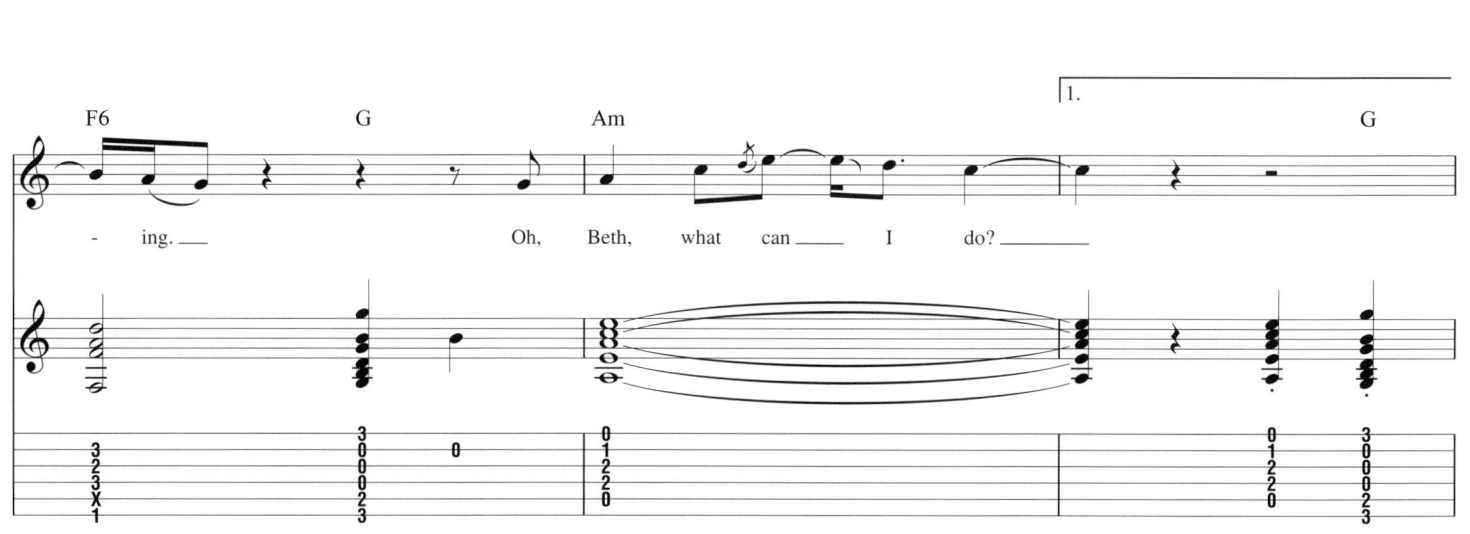

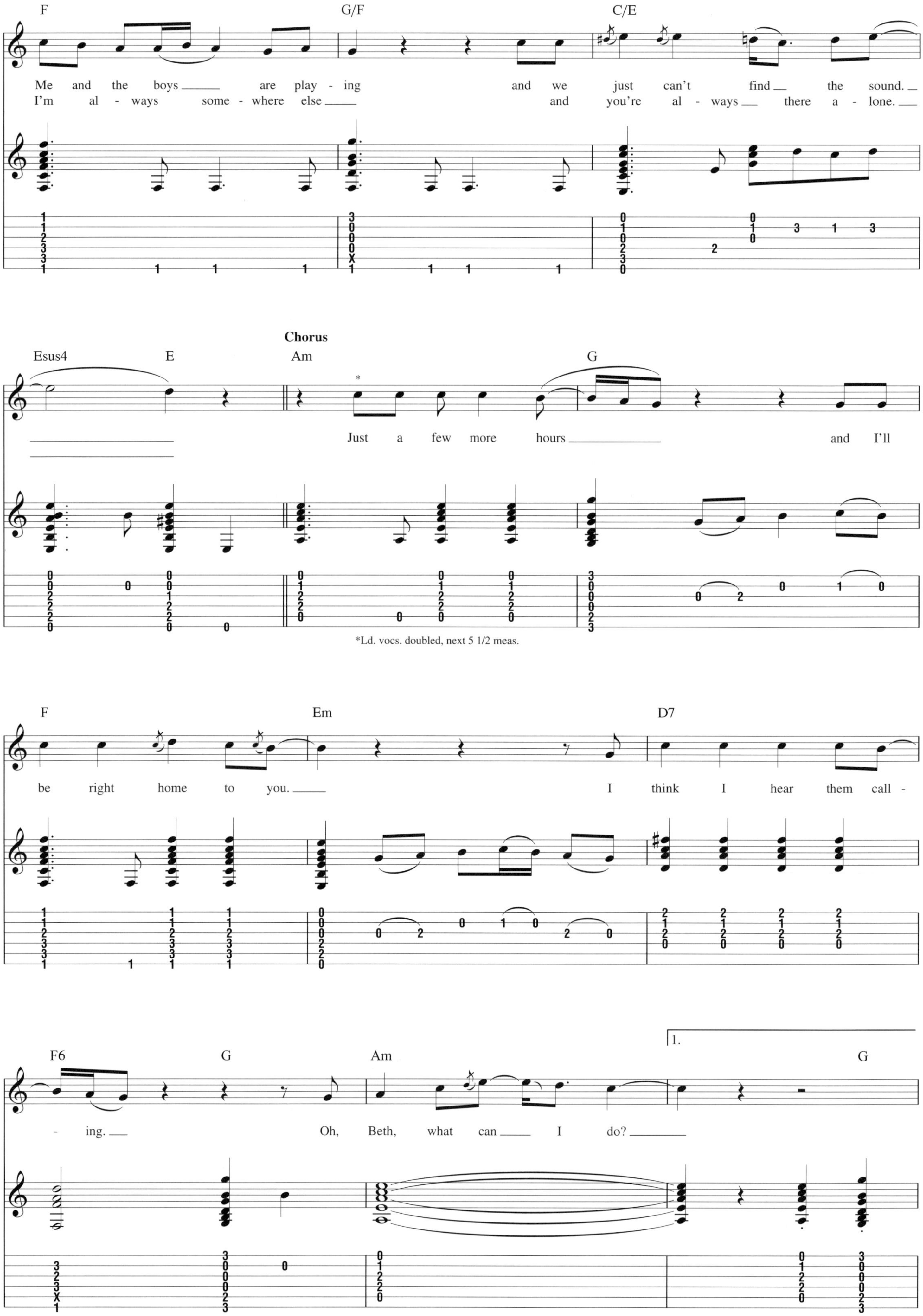
F
G/F
C/E
Me and the boys are play - ing and we just can't find the sound.
I'm al - ways some - where else and you're al - ways there a - lone.
Esus4
E
Chorus
Am
G
Just a few more hours and I'll
*Ld. vocs. doubled, next 5 1/2 meas.
F
Em
D7
be right home to you. I think I hear them call -
F6
G
Am
1.
G
- ing. Oh, Beth, what can I do?

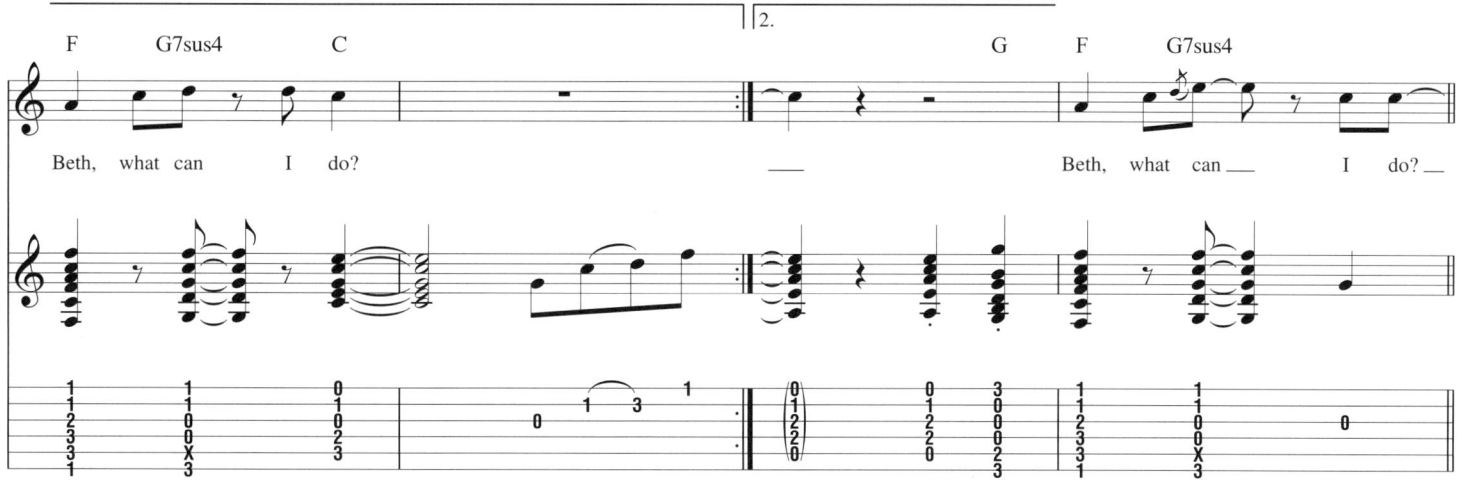

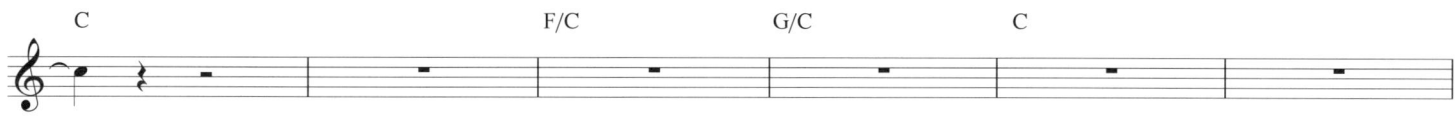

Interlude

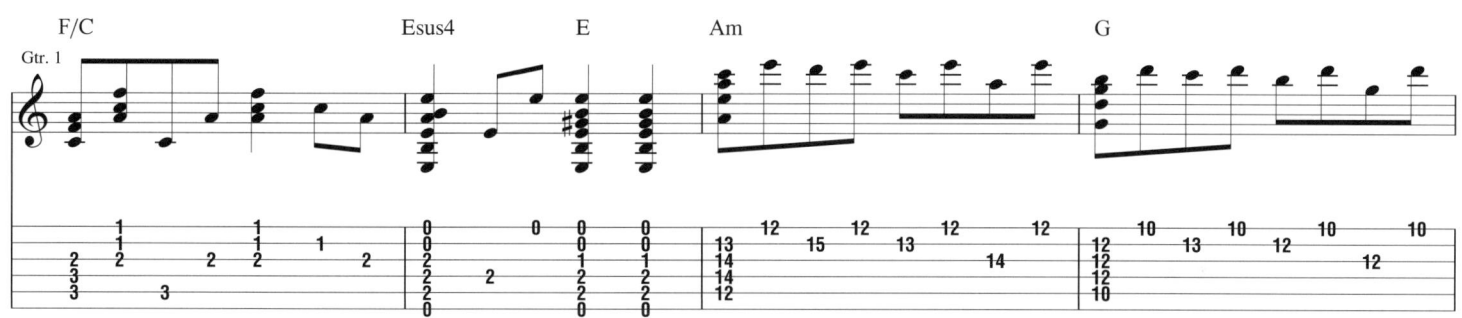

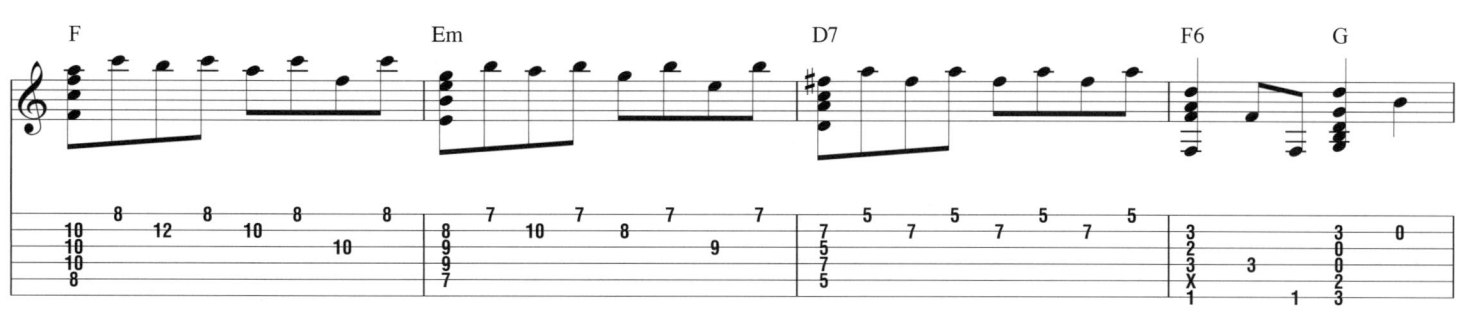

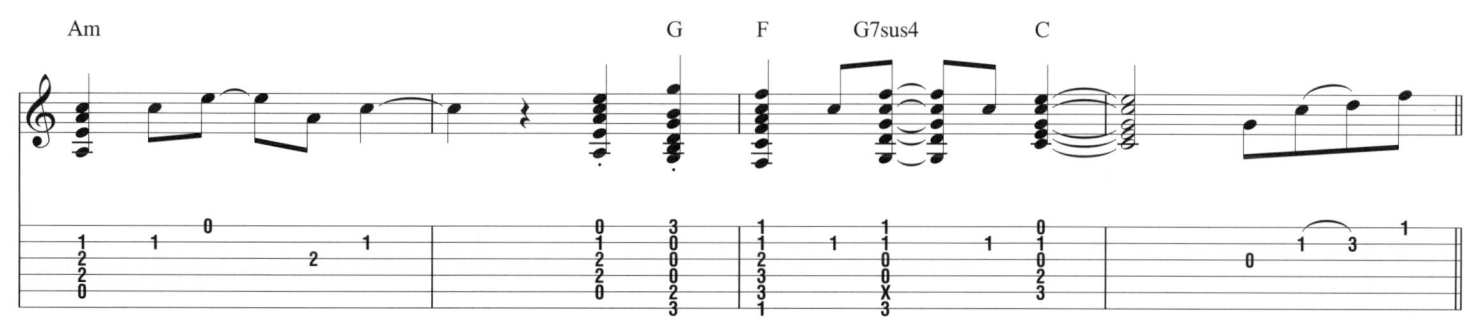

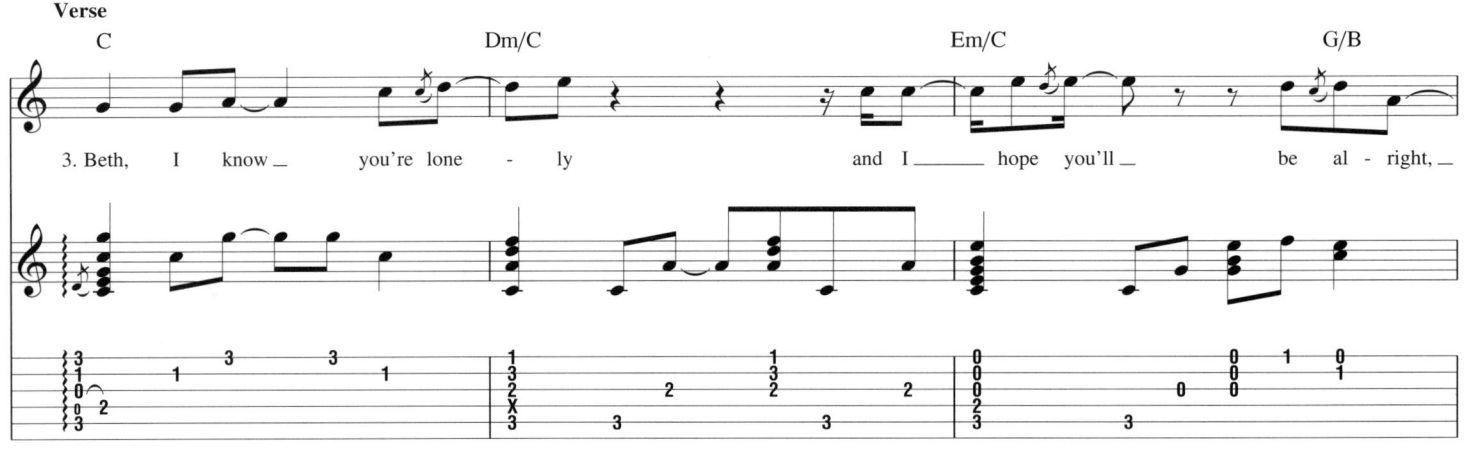
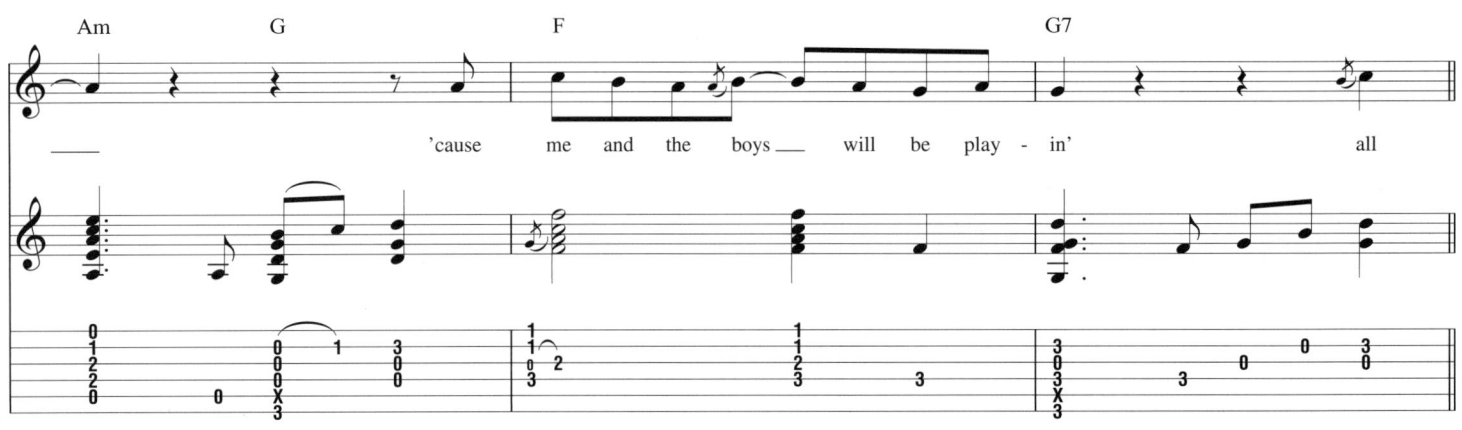
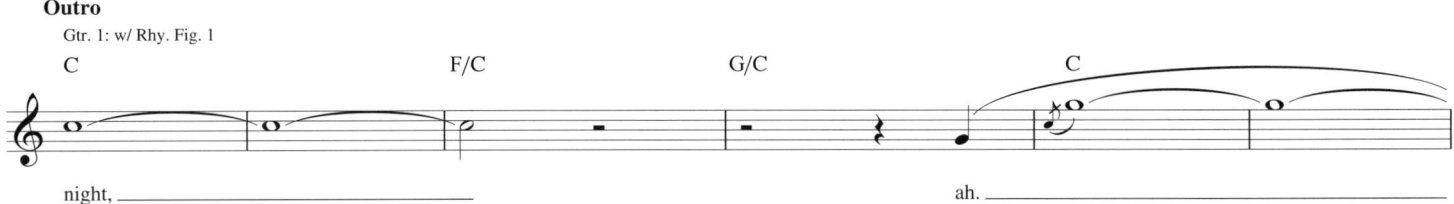
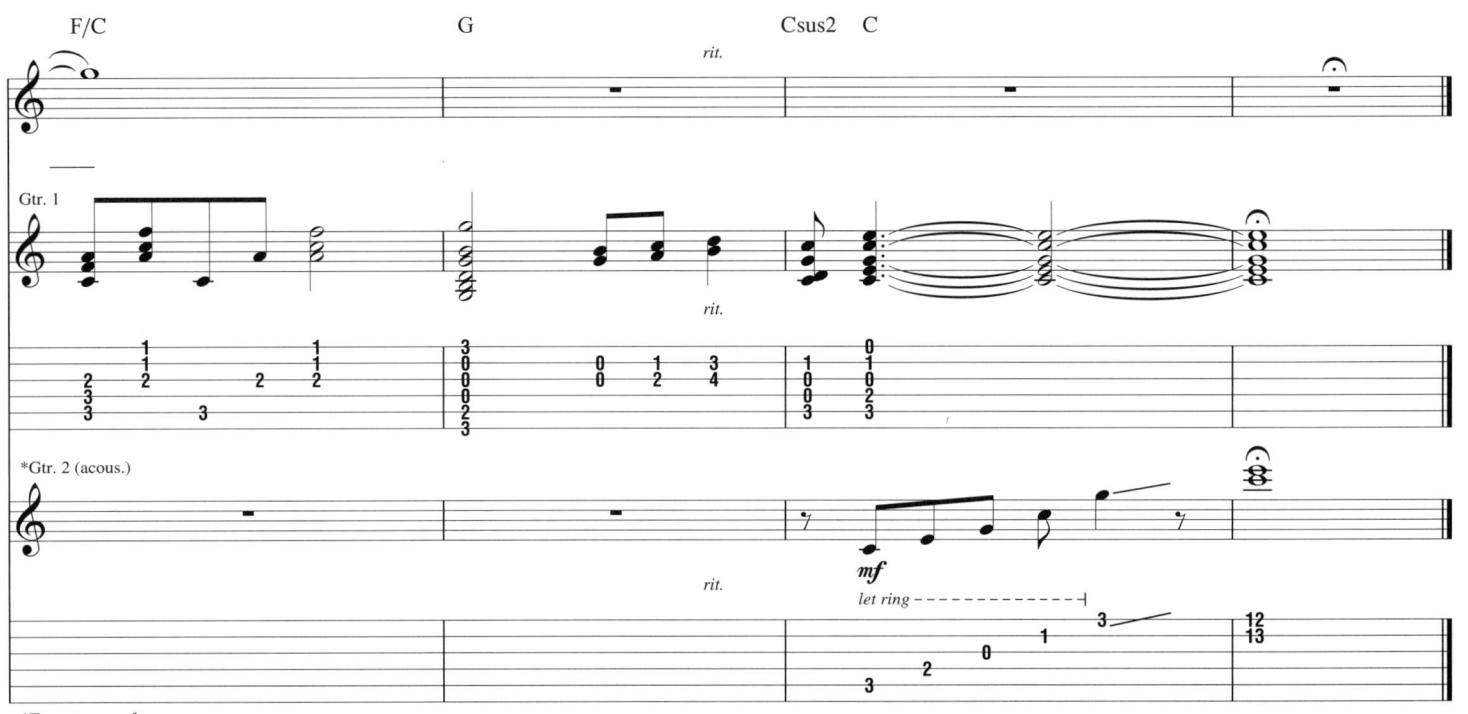

Do You Love Me

Words and Music by Paul Stanley, Bob Ezrin and Kim Fowley

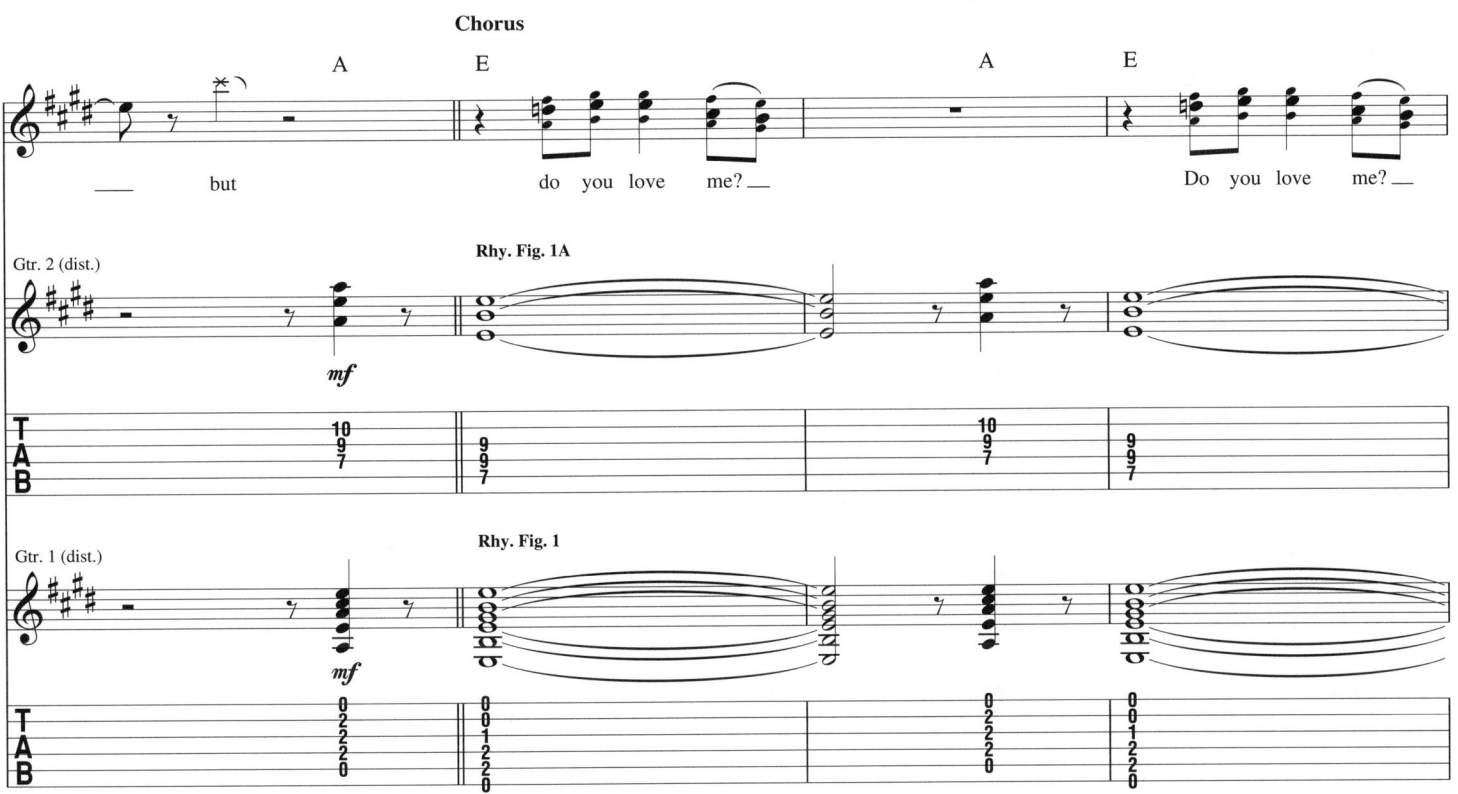

*Chord symbols reflect overall harmony.

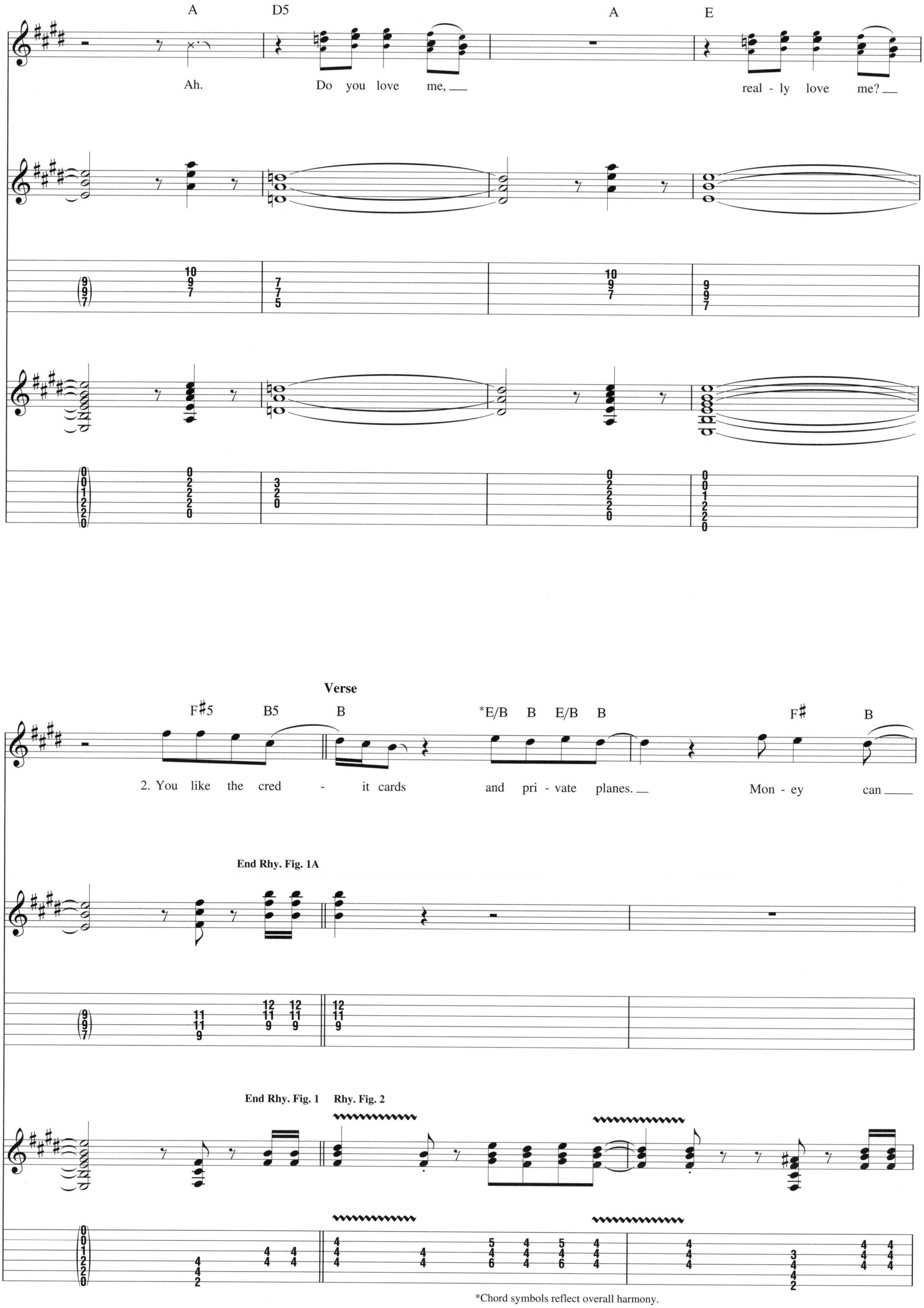

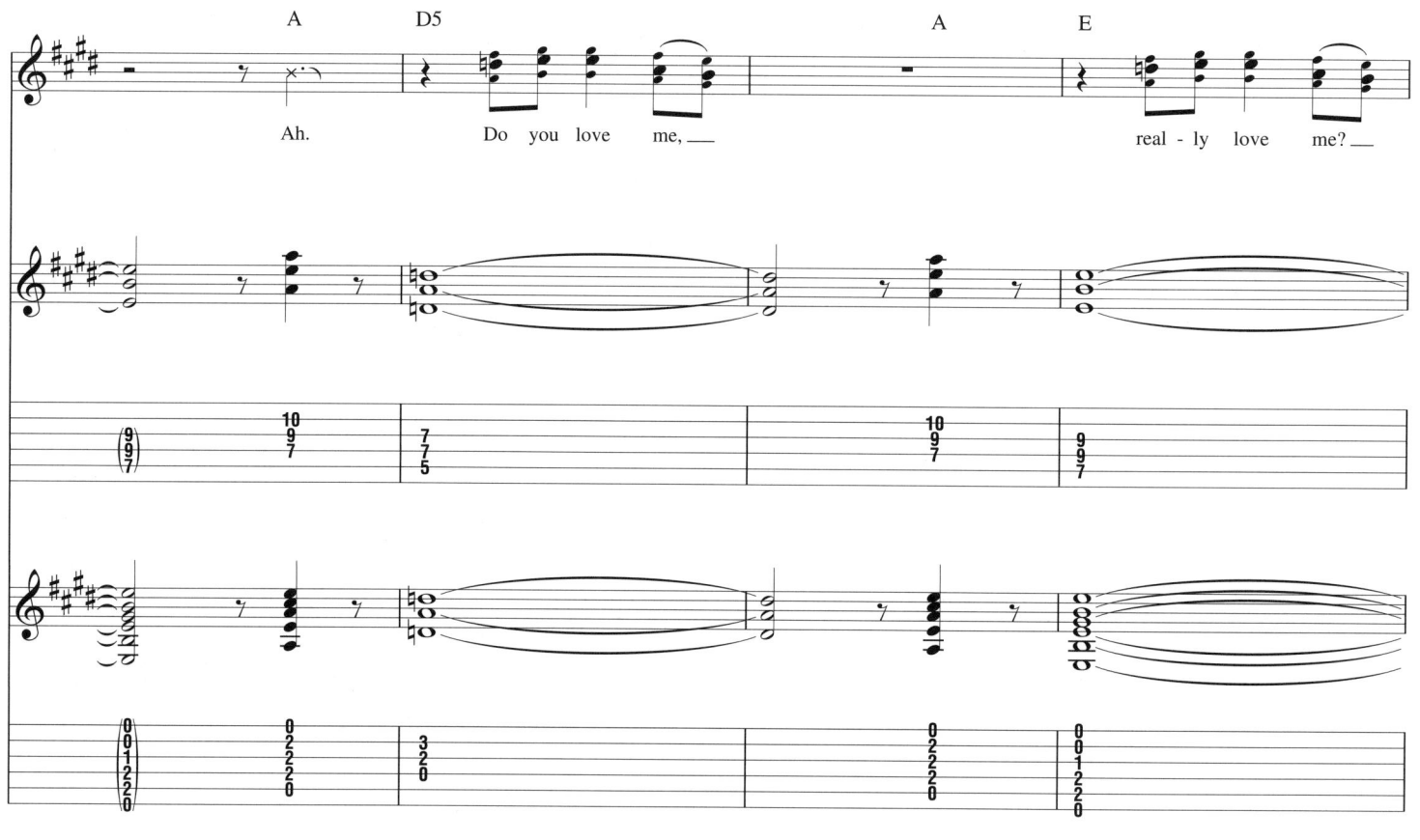

Chorus

Gtr. 1: w/ Rhy. Fig. 1
Gtr. 2: w/ Rhy. Fig. 1A (1st 7 meas.)

Verse

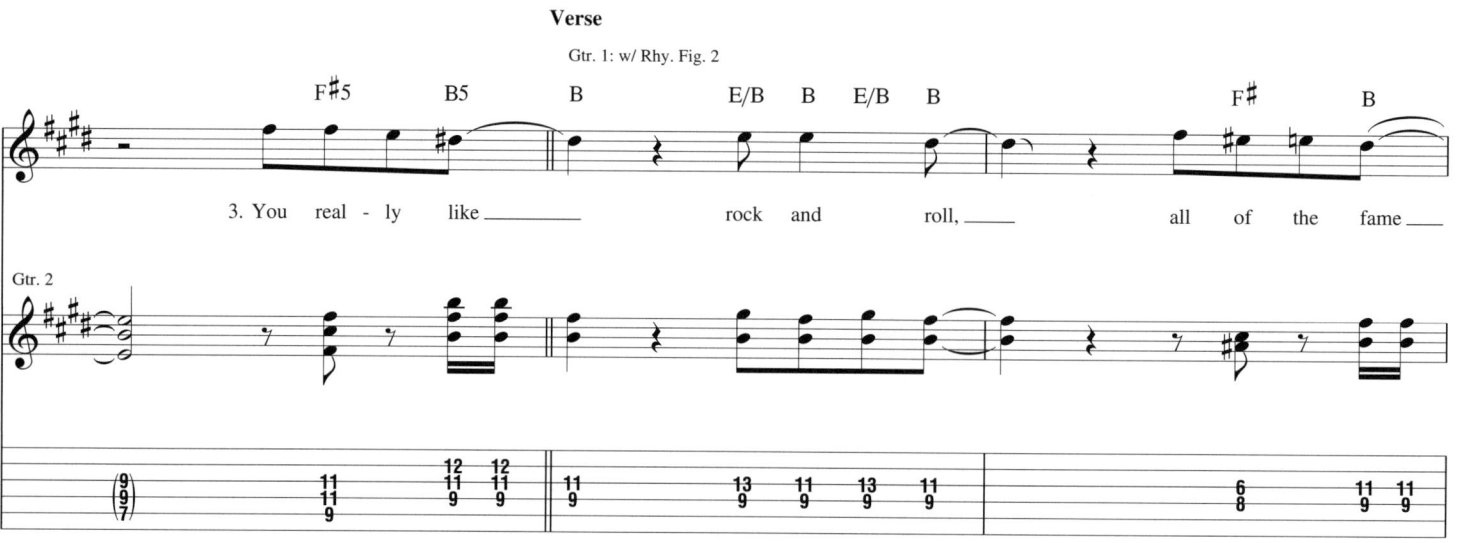

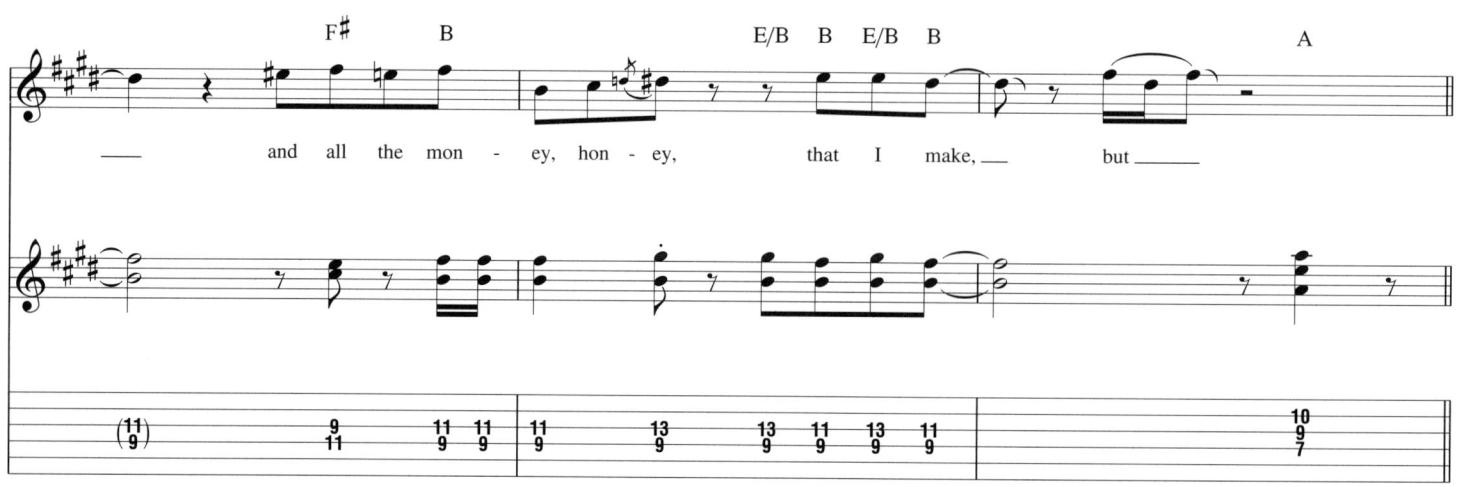

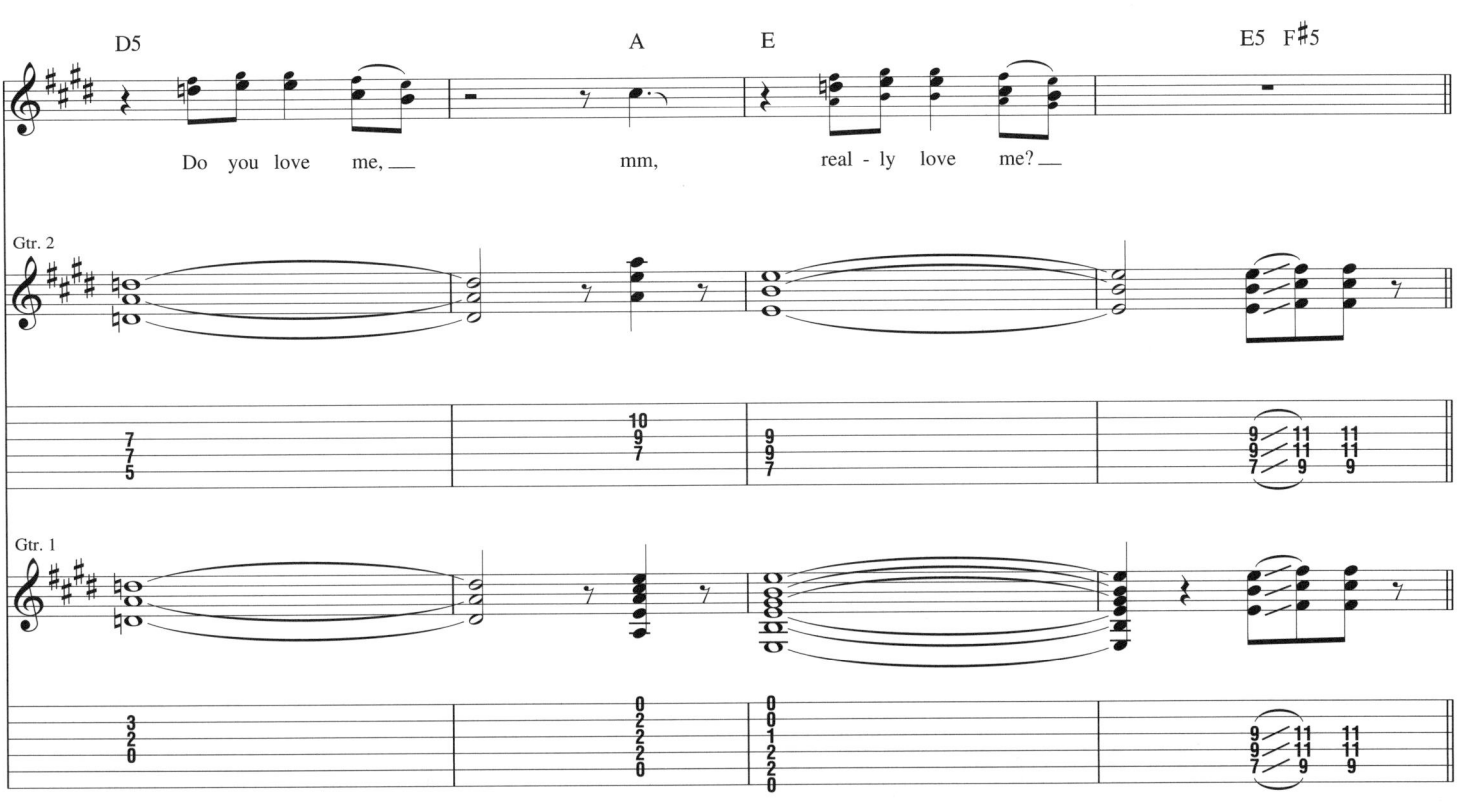

Outro-Chorus

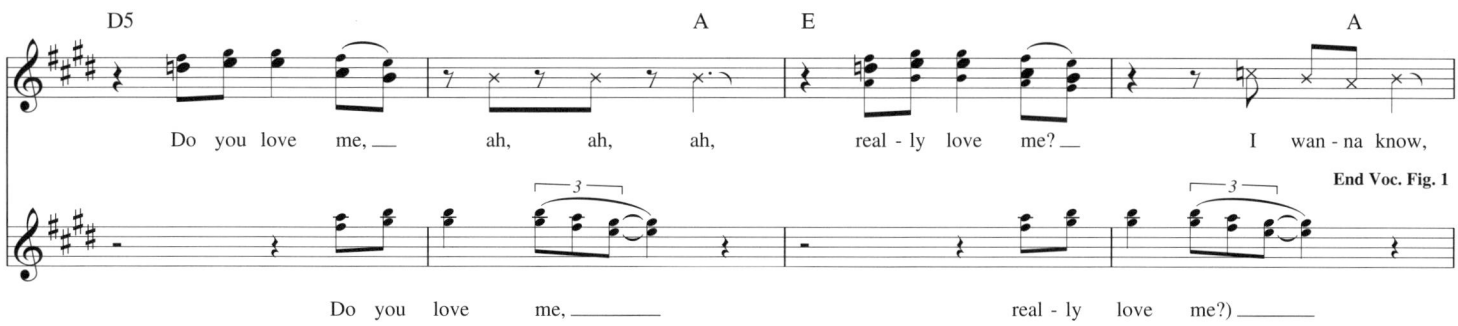

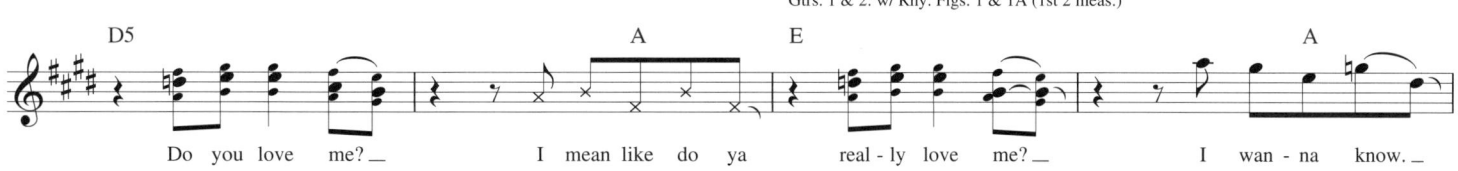
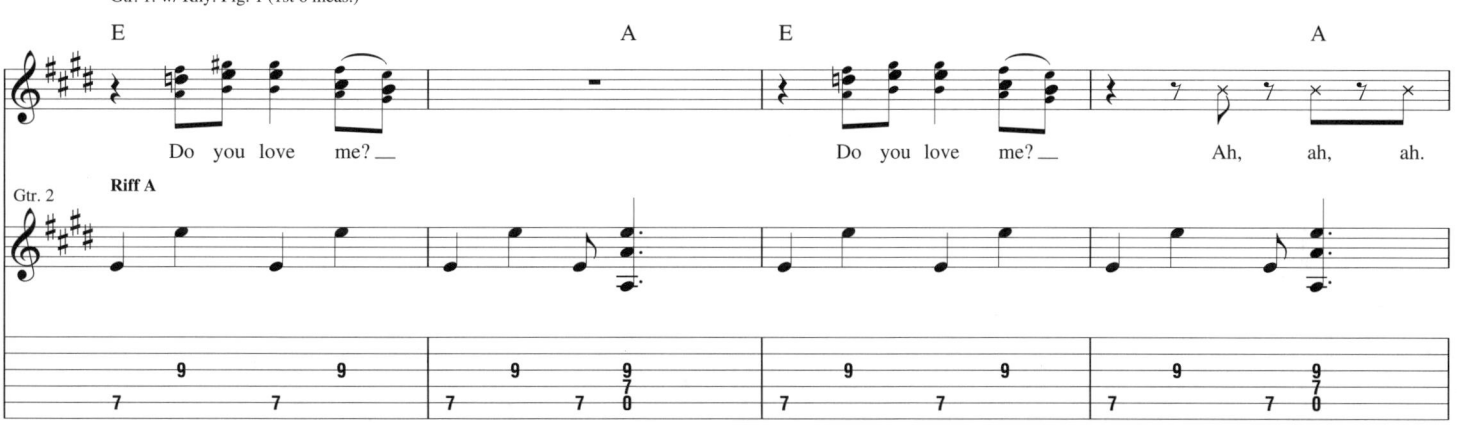

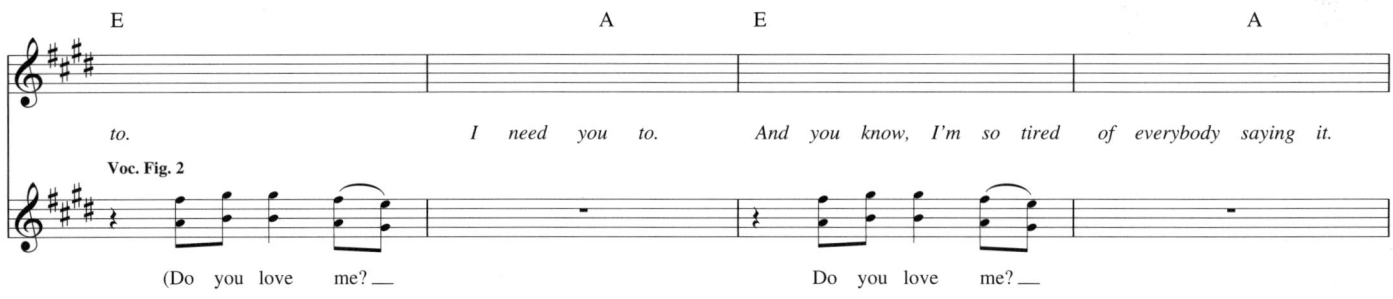
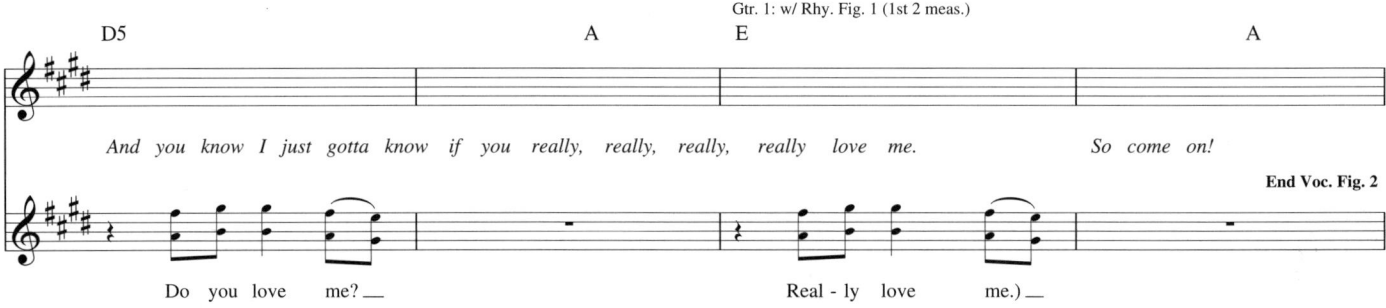

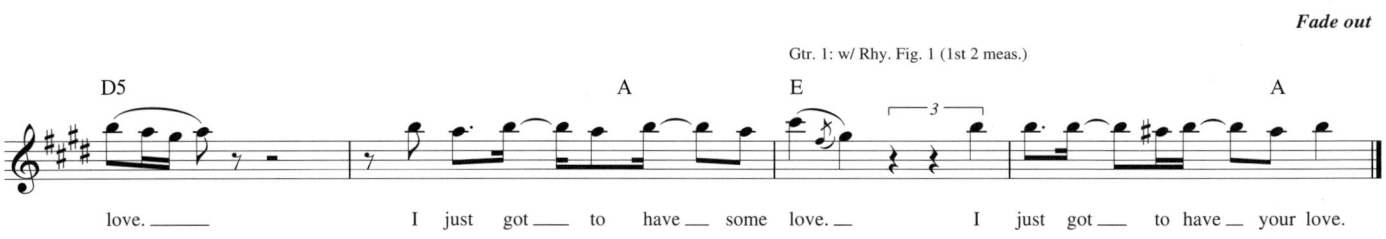